Windows PowerShell Scripting and Toolmaking

Volume 1 • Don Jones

Windows PowerShell
Scripting and Toolmaking

Volume 1

Don Jones

Copyright ©2011 by Don Jones

http://ConcentratedTech.com

for Companion Materials, visit
http://MoreLunches.com

First Printing: October 2011
Available in Print at Lulu.com
Available Electronically through Major eBook Stores

ISBN 978-1-105-08283-2

Cover design by Greg Richard

Published in cooperation with Interface Technical Training
http://InterfaceTT.com

Introduction

Windows PowerShell continues to take the world by storm, showing up in an increasing number of Microsoft and even third-party products.

After the success of my for-beginners PowerShell book, Learn Windows PowerShell in a Month of Lunches, I started receiving requests for a more advanced book. Unfortunately, the more advanced topics don't really lend themselves to the read-it-in-an-hour format of the Lunches series, so I couldn't do a direct sequel. So I wrote this book instead, to at least partially address those more "advanced stuff" requests.

In order to make this a standalone book, I had to overlap a bit with the Lunches book. However, this book definitely tells a story: You'll start with a single project goal, and continue to build upon it throughout the book. By the end, you'll have built a complete set of tools, using only Windows PowerShell, and be able to distribute them to your colleagues.

Before we get started, let's cover some of the typesetting standards I've used in this book.

Typesetting Standards

To make PowerShell commands (and other things you're meant to type into the shell) stand out, I'll set those out in monospaced font, such as `Get-WmiObject`.

Code listings can always be difficult in a book – especially in today's electronic readers, which re-flow text and may cause word-wrapping to occur when it shouldn't. For that reason, I'll present code listings in a line-numbered format:

Listing X-X: An example

```
01 function MyFunction {
02   Get-WmiObject -class Win32_OperatingSystem -computername localhost
03 }
```

Exactly what that looks like will depend upon the font size in your electronic reader. Basically, each numbered line should be typed as a single physical line into your script editor – even if it "wraps" onto multiple lines here in this book. Don't type the line numbers themselves, though.

To help you out, any listing longer than two or three lines will have a listing number ("Listing 1-2," for example), and will be downloadable from http://MoreLunches.com. Just find this book's cover image on the front page, click it, and you'll be taken to a page that offers downloads and other companion resources. I'll include all of the scripts for this entire book in a single ZIP file.

Editing Scripts

I strongly encourage you to obtain a script editor.

While the PowerShell ISE that comes with Windows is fine, it offers a minimal set of features and isn't really suited to the hardcore scripting you'll do in this book. SAPIEN PrimalScript (primalscript.com), Idera PowerShell Plus (idera.com), PowerGUI (powergui.org), and PowerSE (powerwf.com) are all excellent editors. PowerGUI is even available in a free edition. Note that I don't recommend more generic editors that can't also run your scripts. We don't need just editing – we also need the ability to execute the things!

All the script editors I've mentioned offer free trial periods, so you can try them and see which ones you like. They each take a slightly different approach, so it's worth your while to give them a spin to find which ones make the most sense to you.

I don't recommend the use of generic script editors that merely offer syntax coloring. You really need something PowerShell-specific, which offers syntax highlighting, code hinting and completion, and most especially debugging features. PowerGUI, as I've pointed out, is free; you don't need to spend anything to get something that's light-years better than the PowerShell ISE or Notepad.

An Organic Approach

I tend to dislike books that simply feed the correct answers to the reader. In terms of learning something new, there's tremendous value in playing with it, making mistakes and learning from those mistakes. It's the way our brains work, which is why it's sometimes called "organic" learning. Rather than learning like a machine, which expects the correct set of instructions the first time, we as humans tend to learn like... well, like humans, making mistakes and adjusting ourselves appropriately.

This book will definitely follow an organic approach. Because this is a book, and not a live experiment, that approach may sometimes seem artificial. After all, why would I show you the wrong way to do something, when I could just as easily start out by showing you the right way? Because seeing the wrong way is sometimes more valuable. Showing you something that doesn't work, and explaining why, will help you better understand how it works, which will help you better use that something on your own in the future.

So I ask that you trust me, and follow along. Run the commands and scripts that I provide as examples. Don't just take my word for what they do! See it for yourself! Sometimes, things won't work out properly. And when that happens, see if you can figure out why. At the very least, try to form a theory about why something broke. I'll always give you the full explanation, but by at least trying to form a theory on your own, you'll be forcing your brain to analyze what you've done, which helps you learn faster.

This book actually has a single goal: To write our own PowerShell module, not unlike the modules that Microsoft ships with its own products.

Our module will include a few different commands.

One command will use Windows Management Instrumentation (WMI) to retrieve management information from one or more remote computers, in a way that lets the information be easily output to the screen, a file, a CSV file, to XML and so on. We'll make that command look and work as much like a native cmdlet as possible, including providing a customized layout for its output.

We'll write a second command that queries computer names from a database, so that those computer names can be fed to the first command.

A third command will accept the output of the first and save that inventory information back to a database.

We're going to take a while to get to that final goal, because along the way we'll have to learn new techniques, make some mistakes, and adjust our approach accordingly. In the end, you'll have a set of commands that can serve as templates or starting points for your own independent efforts, along with a better understanding of how these advanced PowerShell techniques work.

Welcome to Tier 2

Members of Microsoft's PowerShell team and I tend to describe the PowerShell audience as being broken into three tiers.

Tier 1 consists of the "tool users," the folks who primarily run commands given to them by Microsoft and others. Tier 2 consists of administrators with at least minor programming capability, who re-combine and re-package those tools to automate complete processes within their environment.

This book is designed to make you a Tier 2 user. This book doesn't venture into Tier 3, which is the realm of .NET developers who are extending the shell. That may be an arbitrary line, but it's the line I find most administrators comfortable with. This book will not cross the line into the .NET Framework. We'll work solely with the tools PowerShell gives us.

Sticking with that rule means we won't be able to accomplish some tasks in PowerShell. You're welcome to cross that line yourself if you're comfortable doing so, but this isn't the book that will teach you how.

With that, let's get started.

Acknowledgements

Before we dive in, I'd like to acknowledge a few folks who were instrumental in making this book happen.

First, I want to thank the publisher of Learn Windows PowerShell in a Month of Lunches. The company has been trying to get me to do an advanced PowerShell book for some time, as has fellow MVP Richard Siddaway, who's offered to co-author such a book with me. I still may take them up on that, but this book is a bit too short for a mainstream publisher.

This book was also intended specifically to be a classroom companion, and forms the basis of a "scripting and toolmaking" courseware set and class offered by Interface Technical Training out of Phoenix, Arizona. I'd like to thank Interface for support in creating this book, including editing, technical reviewing and design assistance. Interface Instructors Jason Helmick and Mike Pfeiffer in particular created the labs, slides and other materials needed for a complete courseware set.

I'd also like to acknowledge Apple because most of this book was written on my iPad 2 during a working vacation in Europe in August 2011. Excepting the actual code, which was pasted from a VMware Fusion virtual machine, all of the principal writing took place on the iPad, using Apple's Pages word processor. Amazing stuff. At the same time, I have to thank my partner, Christopher, who was incredibly patient as I wrote on our "vacation." Almost every morning. And on the train. And the ferry. And the next train. You get the idea. If you happen to run into Chris at a conference or event (he runs my business, so he often accompanies me), shake his hand.

Finally, I'd like to thank everyone who's clamored for a book like this. I know, this one isn't all the "advanced" stuff you want. There will be more books, very possibly including a truly advanced title from Manning or another publisher. This at least gets you some of the higher-end material you've asked about. I do appreciate everyone's enthusiasm for PowerShell and their kind words and support for my prior efforts; I promise to try to write whatever you need.

Don Jones, August 2011

Scripting Overview

At this point in your PowerShell education, you should be pretty familiar with the idea of scripting. In this chapter, we'll review some of the more important basics, and briefly cover the major elements of PowerShell's scripting language. We won't cover every single bit of that language; for the bits we don't cover, you can always use PowerShell's built-in help files to learn more and to see examples.

You should also, at this point, have a thorough understanding of PowerShell's security features. You should already know what the execution policy is, and know what setting is in use within your organization. If, for example, you don't already know the difference between "RemoteSigned" and "AllSigned," and why one might be better than the other, then you're not quite ready for the following material. You should also know how to execute scripts in the shell, and should recall that you always have to provide a path and filename in order to execute a script. Finally, you should also know the difference between running a script in the ISE (in which scripts run in the global scope) and in the normal shell console (in which scripts get their own scope). We'll lightly review scope, but you should already have an idea of what it means and what it does.

Essentially, this book assumes that you've read all the way through Learn Windows PowerShell in a Month of Lunches, and that you've completed its hands-on exercises – or that you've taken a 3- or 4-day course that's the equivalent of that book. You'll find a bit of repeated information in this book – such as error handling and debugging – although in most cases those topics will be covered in greater depth, with a focus on the "gotchas" that tend to trip you up once you start actually using them.

PowerShell Script Files

A PowerShell script file is nothing more than a plain-text file that has a .PS1 filename extension. The "1" doesn't refer to the version of PowerShell, but rather to the version of the language engine used by the shell. Both PowerShell v1 and v2 use language engine v1, which is also why both versions of the shell are installed into a "v1.0" folder under \Windows\System32\WindowsPowerShell.

A PowerShell script isn't exactly like a command-line batch file, and running a script isn't precisely the same as running the same commands yourself in the same sequence. For example, open a console window and run the following, pressing Enter after each line (remember not to type the line numbers):

Listing 2-1

```
01 Get-Service
04 Get-Process
```

Now type those exact same lines into a script file, or into the ISE's script editing pane, and run the script. You'll get different-looking results.

In PowerShell, each time you hit Enter you start a new pipeline. The commands you typed are run in that single pipeline, and at the end of the pipeline PowerShell converts the contents of the pipeline into a text display. When you run the two commands in the normal console, you did so in two distinct pipelines. Therefore, PowerShell was able to construct a unique display for each set of output. When entered into a script, however, both commands ran in the same pipeline, and PowerShell's formatting system isn't sophisticated enough to construct the same unique output for two different sets of results. Try running this in the console:

Two Commands on One Line

```
01 Get-Service;Get-Process
```

Those results should look the same as they did when you ran the script containing those two commands. That's because in this case, both commands ran in a single pipeline, which is what happened when you ran the script.

The practical upshot of all this is that a script should produce one kind of output only. It's a bad idea – due in large part to the limitations of the formatting system, but also due to other considerations – to have a script that's dumping several different kinds of things into the pipeline at the same time.

Focus on that as a rule for everything that we'll cover: A script should output one, and only one, kind of thing.

Variables

Think of variables as a box, into which you can put one or more things, even dissimilar things. The box has a name, and in PowerShell that name can include almost anything. "Var" can be a variable name, as can "{my variable}". In that second example, the curly brackets enclose a variable name that contains spaces, which is pretty ugly. As a good practice, stick with variable names that include letters, numbers, and underscores.

Using a variable's name references the entire "box," but if you want to reference the contents of the box you add a dollar sign: $var. Most commonly, you'll see PowerShell variables preceded with the dollar sign because the whole point of using one is to get at the contents. It's important to remember, however, that the dollar sign isn't part of the variable name: It's just a cue to tell PowerShell that you want the contents, rather than the box itself.

Placing Objects in Variables

```
01 $var = 'hello'
05 $number = 1
06 $numbers = 1,2,3,4,5,6,7,8,9
```

Those examples show how to place items into a variable, by using the assignment operator (=). Note, the third example creates an array because PowerShell interprets all comma-separated lists as an array, or collection, of items. The first example assigns a string object, with the characters in the string contained within quotation marks.

One thing that can sometimes confuse newcomers: PowerShell doesn't "understand" any meaning you may associate with a variable name. A variable like $computername doesn't "tell" the shell that the variable will contain a computer name. Similarly, $numbers doesn't "tell" the shell that a variable will contain more than one number – the shell doesn't care if you use a variable name that happens to be plural. $numbers = 1 is equally valid to the shell, as is $numbers = 'fred.'

When a variable does contain multiple values, however, you can use a special syntax to access just a single one of them. $numbers[0] gets the first item, $numbers[1] is the second, $numbers[-1] is the last, $numbers[-2] is the second-last, and so on.

Quotation Marks

As a best practice, you should use single quotes to delimit a variable unless you have a specific reason not to. There are three specific instances where you would want to use double quotes.

The first is when you need to insert a variable's contents into a string. Within double quotes only, PowerShell will look for the $, and will assume that everything after the $, up to the first character that's illegal in a variable name, is a variable name. The variable name and $ will be replaced with the contents of that variable.

Double Quotes Replace Variables

```
01 $name = 'Don'
02 $prompt = "My name is $name"
```

$prompt will now contain "My name is Don" because $name will be replaced with the contents of the variable. This is a great trick for joining strings together without having to concatenate them.

Within double quotes, PowerShell will also look for its escape character, the backtick or grave accent, and act accordingly. Here are a couple of examples:

Double Quotes Use Escape Characters

```
01 $debug = "`$computer contains $computer"
02 $head = "Column`tColumn`tColumn"
```

In the first example, the first $ is being escaped. That removes its special meaning as a variable accessor, so if $computer contained 'SERVER' then $debug will contain "$computer contains SERVER". In the second example, `t represents a horizontal tab character, so PowerShell will place a tab between each "Column". You can read about other special escape characters in the shell's about_escape_characters help topic.

Finally, use double quotes when a string needs to contain single quotes.

Double Quotes Contain Single Quotes

```
01 $filter1 = "name='BITS'"
02 $computer = 'BITS'
03 $filter2 = "name='$computer'"
```

In this example, the literal string is name='BITS' and the double quotes contain the whole thing. Both $filter1 and $filter2 end up containing exactly the same thing; $filter2 gets there by using the variable-replacement trick of double quotes. Note that only the outermost set of quotes matters when it comes to that trick – the fact that single quotes are used within the string doesn't matter to PowerShell. Those single quotes are just literal characters; PowerShell doesn't interpret them.

Object Members and Variables

Everything in PowerShell is an object. Even a simple string like 'name' is an object, of the type System.String. You can pipe any object to Get-Member to see its type name (that is, the kind of object it is) as well as its members, which includes its properties and methods.

Using Get-Member with a Variable

```
01 $var = 'Hello'
02 $var | Get-Member
```

Use a period after a variable name to tell the shell, "I don't want to access the entire object within this variable; I want to access just one of its properties or methods." After the period, provide the property or method name. Method names are always followed by (parentheses). Some methods accept input arguments, and those go within the parentheses in a comma-separated list. Other methods require no arguments, and so the parentheses are empty. But don't forget the parentheses!

Working With Object Members

```
01 $svc = Get-Service
02 $svc[0].name
03 $name = $svc[1].name
04 $name.length
05 $name.ToUpper()
```

Notice line 2. It starts by accessing the first item in the $svc variable. The period means, "I don't want that entire object – I just want a property or method." We've then accessed just the name property. Line 5 illustrates how to access a method, by providing its name after a period, and then following that with the parentheses.

A period is normally an illegal character within a variable name, because the period means we want to access a property or method. That means line 2, below, won't work the way you might expect.

Accessing Members Within Quotes

```
01 $service = 'bits'
02 $name = "Service is $service.ToUpper()"
03 $upper = $name.ToUpper()
04 $name = "Service is $upper"
```

On line 2, $name will contain "Service is BITS.ToUpper()" whereas on line 4 $name will contain "Service is BITS".

Parentheses

Aside from their use with object methods, parentheses also act as an order-of-execution marker for PowerShell. In other words, just as in algebra, parentheses tell the shell to "execute this first." The entire parenthetical expression is replaced by whatever that expression produced. Here are a couple of mind-bending examples:

Using Parentheses

```
01 $name = (Get-Service)[0].name
02 Get-Service -computerName (Get-Content names.txt)
```

On line 1, $name will contain the name of the first service on the system. Reading this takes a bit of effort: Start with the parenthetical expression, because that's what PowerShell will start with as well. Get-Service resolves to a collection, or array, of services. [0] will access the first item in an array, so that'll be the first service. Followed by a period, we know that we're accessing a property or method of that service, rather than the entire service object. Finally, we pull out just the name of the service.

On line 2, the parenthetical expression is reading the contents of a text file. Assuming that file contains one computer name per line, Get-Content returns an array of computer names. Those are fed to the -computerName parameter of Get-Service. Any parenthetical expression that returns an array of strings can be fed to the -computerName parameter in this case, because the parameter is designed to accept arrays of strings.

Scope

Scope is a programming concept, and acts as a kind of containerization system. Things like variables, aliases, PSDrives and other PowerShell elements are all stored in a scope. The shell maintains a hierarchy of scopes, and has a set of rules that determine how scopes can interact and share information with each other.

The shell itself is a single scope, called the global scope. When you run a script, a new scope is constructed and the script runs within it. Anything created by the script – such as a new variable – is stored within the script's scope, and is not accessible by the top-level shell. When the script finishes running, its scope is discarded, and anything created within that scope disappears. For example, create a script that contains the following (don't forget not to type the line numbers), and then run that script from the console window:

```
01 New-PSDrive -PSProvider FileSystem -Root C:\ -Name Sys
02 Dir SYS:
```

After running the script, manually run Dir SYS: and you should see an error. That's because the SYS: drive was created in the script. Once the script was done, everything it created was discarded – so the SYS: drive no longer exists. Not everything in the shell is scoped; things like modules are handled globally at all times, so that a script can load a module and the module will remain loaded after the script is done.

If a scope tries to access something that hasn't been created in it, then PowerShell looks to the next-higher scope (the "parent" scope) for that item. That's why the Dir alias worked in that script you just entered: Although Dir didn't exist in the script's scope, it did exist in the next-higher scope, which was the global scope. However, a scope is free to create an item that has the same name as an item from a higher-level scope. Here's another script to try:

```
01 Dir
02 New-Alias Dir Get-Alias
03 Dir
```

Weird, right? The first time Dir was run, it didn't exist in the script's scope, and so the higher-level Dir alias was used. That alias points to Get-ChildItem, and so a familiar directory listing was displayed. Then, the script creates a new alias named Dir, which points to Get-Alias. That's what was run the second time. None of this affected the top-level Dir alias; try running Dir in the shell, after running the above script, and you'll still get a directory listing.

This scope thing can be especially confusing when it comes to variables. As a rule, a given scope should never access out-of-scope items, especially variables. There's a syntax for doing so, such as using $global:var to forcibly access the global scope's $var variable, but it's a bad programming practice except under very specific circumstances. We'll discuss those specific circumstances later in this book.

PowerShell Scripting Language

PowerShell contains a very simplified scripting language of less than two dozen keywords – that's a stark contrast with full programming language like VBScript, which contains almost 300 keywords. Simplified though it may be, PowerShell's language is more than sufficient to get the job done. We'll review its major scripting constructs now, although you can always get more help on these by reading the appropriate "about" topic within the shell. For example, help about_switch contains information on the Switch construct, while help about_if contains information on the If construct. Run help about* for a list of all "about" topics.

If Construct

This is PowerShell's main decision-making construct. In its full form, it looks like this:

If Example

```
01 If ($this -eq $that) {
02   # commands
03 } elseif ($those -ne $them) {
04   # commands
05 } elseif ($we -gt $they) {
06   # commands
07 } else {
08   # commands
09 }
```

The If keyword is a mandatory part of this construct. Following it is a parenthetical expression that must evaluate to either True or False – although PowerShell will always interpret 0 (zero) as False, and any nonzero value as True. PowerShell also recognizes the built-in variables $True and $False as representing those Boolean values. If the expression in parentheses works out to True, the commands in the following set of curly brackets will execute. If the expression is False, the commands won't execute. That's really all you need for a valid If construct.

However, you can go a bit further by providing one or more ElseIf sections. These work the same way: They get their own parenthetical expression, and if that's True, the commands within the following curly brackets will execute. If not, they won't.

Finally, you can wrap up with an Else block, which will execute if none of the preceding blocks executed. Only the block associated with the first True expression will execute. For example, if $this did not equal $that, and $those did not equal $them, then the commands on line 4 would execute – and nothing else. PowerShell won't even evaluate the second ElseIf expression on line 5.

Note that the # character is a comment character, making PowerShell essentially ignore anything from there until a carriage return.

Also notice the care with which those constructs were formatted. You might also see formatting like this from some folks:

Alternate Construct Formatting

```
01 if ($those -eq $these)
02 {
03    #commands
04 }
```

It doesn't matter where you place the curly brackets. However, what does matter is that you be consistent about how you place them, so that your scripts are easier to read. It's also important to indent, to the exact same level, every line within the curly brackets. The PowerShell ISE lets you use the Tab key for that purpose, and it defaults to a 4-character indent. Indenting your code is a core best practice – fail to do so and you'll have a tough time properly matching opening and closing curly brackets in complex scripts. Also, all of the other PowerShell kids out there will make fun of you. Deservedly. Imagine looking a script that's poorly formatted:

Don't Get Caught Doing This

```
01 function mine {
02 if ($this -eq $that){
03 get-service
04 }}
```

That's a lot harder to read, to debug, to troubleshoot, and to maintain. While the space after the closing parentheses isn't necessary, it does make your script easier to read. The indented code isn't necessary, but it makes your script easier to follow. Placing a single closing curly bracket on a line by itself isn't required by the shell, but it's appreciated by human eyes. Be a neat formatter, and you'll have fewer problems in your scripts. And in your life.

Do...While Construct

This is a looping construct in PowerShell. It's designed to repeat a block of commands so long as some condition is True, or until a condition becomes True. Here's the basic usage:

Do...While Example

```
01 Do {
02   # commands
03 } While ($this -eq $that)
```

In this variation of the construct, the commands within the curly brackets will always execute at least one time, because the While condition isn't evaluated until after the first execution. You can move the While, in which case the commands will only execute if the condition is True in the first place:

Do...While Example 2

```
01 While (Test-Path $path) {
02   # commands
03 }
```

This second example doesn't use a comparison operator like -eq. That's because the Test-Path cmdlet happens to return True or False to begin with; there's no need to compare that to True or False in order for the expression to work. The parenthetical expression used with these scripting constructs merely needs to simplify down to True or False – if you're using a command like Test-Path, which always returns True or False, then that's all you need.

As always, there's an "about" topic in the shell that demonstrates other ways to use this construct.

ForEach Construct

This construct is very similar in operation to the ForEach-Object cmdlet, and differs only in its syntax. The purpose of ForEach is to take an array (or collection, which in PowerShell is the same as an array) and enumerate the objects in the array so that you can work with one at a time.

ForEach Example

```
01 $services = Get-Service
02 ForEach ($service in $services) {
03   $service.Stop()
04 }
```

It's easy for newcomers to overthink this construct. Here are a few things to remember:

- The fact that $services happens to be a plural English word doesn't mean anything at all to PowerShell. That variable name is used to remind us, as human beings, that the variable contains one or more services. Just because it's plural doesn't make the shell behave in a special fashion.

- The "in" keyword on line 2 is part of the ForEach syntax.

- The $service variable is one I made up. It could as easily have been $fred or $coffee and it would have worked in just the same way.

- PowerShell will repeat the construct's commands – the ones contained within curly brackets – one time for each object that's in the second variable ($services). Each time, a single object will be taken from the second variable ($services) and placed into the first variable ($service).

- Within the construct, use the first variable ($service) to work with an individual object. On line 3, I've used the period to indicate that I don't want to work with the entire object, but would like to work with one of its members – the Stop() method.

There are times when using ForEach is inevitable and even desirable. However, if you have a bit of programming or scripting in your past, you can sometimes leap to using ForEach when it isn't the best approach. The example above isn't a good reason to use ForEach. Wouldn't this be easier?

Rather Than ForEach...

```
01 Get-Service | Stop-Service
```

The point here is to evaluate your use of ForEach and make sure it's the only way to accomplish what you're trying to do. In these instances, ForEach is probably the only way to go:

- When you need to execute a method against a bunch of objects, and there's no cmdlet that performs the equivalent action.

- When you have a bunch of objects and need to perform several consecutive actions against each one.

- When you have an action that can only be performed against one object at a time, but your script may be working with one or more objects, and you have no way of knowing in advance.

Other Constructs

PowerShell has several other scripting constructs, including Switch, For, and so on. These are all documented in "about" help topics within the shell, and you're on your own for reviewing these. You won't find them used much throughout the rest of this book.

Sometimes, these other constructs can be replaced with one covered here. Switch can generally be replaced with an If construct that uses multiple ElseIf sections. For can be replaced with ForEach, or even with the ForEach-Object cmdlet. The following is an example of having a loop that executes exactly ten times:

Alternative to For

```
01 1..10 | ForEach-Object -process {
02    # code here will repeat 10 times
03    # use $_ to access the current iteration
04    # number
05 }
```

It's up to you how to do this type of thing; if you're browsing the Internet for scripts, be prepared to run across any and all variations!

Functions

A function is a special kind of construct, used to contain a group of related commands that perform some single, specific task. Generally speaking, you can take any PowerShell script and "wrap" it in a function.

Example Function

```
01 function Mine {
02    Get-Service
03    Get-Process
04 }
05 Mine
```

This defines a new function called "Mine." That basically turns "Mine" into a command, meaning you can run the function simply by entering its name. In fact, that's what line 5 does – it runs the function. You'll see a lot more functions used throughout the rest of this book.

Functions are typically contained within a script file, and a single script can contain multiple functions. Functions can themselves contain other functions. Functions are, however, scoped items. That means a function can only be used within the same scope as it was created in. If you put a function into a script, and then run that script, the function will only be available within the script and only for the duration of the script. When the script finishes running, the function – like everything else in the script's scope – goes away. Consider this example:

Listing 1-1: What Will Happen Here?

```
01 function One {
02    function Two {
```

```
03      Dir
04    }
05    Two
06 }
07 One
08 Two
```

Suppose you enter this all into a single script file, and then run that script. Line 7 executes the function One, which starts on line 1. Line 5 executes a function named Two, which starts on line 2. So the result will be a directory listing, which is on line 3 inside function Two. However, the next line to execute will be line 8, and that will result in an error. The script does not contain a function named Two. Function Two is buried inside function One, and as a result exists within function One's scope. Only other things within function One can see Two; attempting to call Two from anyplace else will result in an error.

Adding Parameters to a Script

It's rare to create a script that's intended to do exactly the same thing every time you run it. More frequently, you'll have scripts that contain some kind of variable data, like computer names to run against, or variable behavior, such as creating a log file sometimes, while other times not doing so. These variations are accommodated through the use of parameters.

When used, parameters are defined in a special way at the top of the script. This definition can be preceded by comments, if you like, but must otherwise be the first executable lines of code within the script. Within the parameter definition area, each parameter is separated from the next by a comma. In keeping with the idea of neat formatting, I like to place each parameter on a line of its own. Here is an example:

Parameter Definition

```
01 param (
02    [string]$computername,
03    [string]$logfile,
04    [int]$attemptcount = 5
05 )
```

This example defines three parameters. Within the script, these are simply used like any other variable. You'll notice that on line 4, I assigned a default value to the $attemptcount parameter. The default will be overridden by any input parameter, but will be used if the script is run without that parameter being specified. Here are several ways in which the script might be run, assuming I saved it as Test.ps1:

Specifying Parameters

```
01 ./test -computername SERVER
02 ./test -comp SERVER -log err.txt -attempt 2
03 ./test SERVER err.txt 2
04 ./test SERVER 2
05 ./test -log err.txt -attempt 2 -comp SERVER
```

In other words, the script accepts parameters pretty much like a cmdlet does. My variable names are used as the parameter names, specified with the usual dash that precedes all parameters names in PowerShell.

On line 1, I'm only specifying one of the parameters. $logfile will thus be empty, and $attemptcount will contain 5, its default.

On line 2, I'm specifying all three parameters, although I'm doing so using shortened parameter names. As with cmdlets, you only need to type enough of the parameter name for PowerShell to know which one you're talking about.

Line 3 shows me again specifying all three parameters, although I'm doing so positionally, without using parameter names. As long as I remember to provide values in the exact order in which the parameters are listed in the script, this will work fine.

Line 4 shows what happens if you're not careful. Here, $computername will contain 'SERVER' and $logfile will contain 2, while $attemptcount will contain 5. That's probably not what I intended, but when you don't use parameter names, you make it more difficult to be flexible. It's also harder for others to decode what you meant, which makes it harder for them to troubleshoot any problems.

Line 5 is a better example. Here, I've specified parameters out-of-order, but that's fine because I used their parameter names. As a general rule, I always use parameter names because doing so gives me the greatest flexibility: I don't need to remember what order they come in.

Advanced Scripts

PowerShell supports a technique for specifying additional information about parameters. This lets you declare a parameter is being mandatory, as accepting input from the pipeline, and so forth. This technique is called Cmdlet Binding. It doesn't change the way in which the parameters are used within a script; it simply gives the shell a bit more information about the parameters. You'll find this technique more commonly used in a function, but the syntax is valid within a script as well. Here's a simple example:

Advanced Parameters

```
01 [CmdletBinding()]
02 param (
03   [Parameter(Mandatory=$True)]
04   [string]$computername,
05
06   [Parameter(Mandatory=$True)]
07   [string]$logfile,
08
09   [int]$attemptcount = 5
10 )
```

All I've done is add the [CmdletBinding()] instruction as the first
executable line of code within the script (it's okay for comments to
precede this, but nothing else may), and added a [Parameter()]
instruction to two of my parameters. Within that [Paramater()]
instruction, I've simply indicated that these parameters are mandatory.
Now, if someone tries to run the script without specifying these
parameters, PowerShell will prompt them for the information. Notice that
the last parameter doesn't have any special instructions associated with it,
and that all three parameters still appear in a comma-separated list
(meaning the first two parameters are followed by commas). There are a
ton of other instructions you can specify for a parameter, but we'll cover
those in combination with Advanced Functions, which is where they're
more usually seen.

Conclusion
This was a whirlwind review of some key PowerShell scripting-related
concepts. Hopefully, much of this information was already in your head. If
you picked up a few new things, great! If a lot of this looked new to you,
then you're probably not quite ready to proceed with the rest of this book.
Spend some time learning more about these concepts first – my book,
Learn Windows PowerShell in a Month of Lunches would be a good start.
From here, we'll dive into more advanced material, starting with functions
that fully utilized the Cmdlet Binding style of parameter. You may have
seen, or even used, this kind of function before – but we're going to dive
into them in a much greater level of detail.

Advanced Functions

PowerShell actually contains three distinct types of functions: Basic, Filtering, and Advanced. We'll basically ignore the first two kinds (they're covered in pretty good detail in Learn Windows PowerShell in a Month of Lunches), and just head straight for the good stuff. You'll see some examples of basic functions later in this book, but your goal should always be to create advanced functions because they're more consistent with the shell's own native commands.

Advanced Function Template

Here's a template to get you started with advanced functions:

Listing 2-1: Advanced Function Template

```
01 function <name> {
02   [CmdletBinding()]
03   param (
04     [Parameter()]<type><name>,
05     [Parameter()]<type><name>,
06     ...
07   )
08   BEGIN {}
09   PROCESS {}
10   END {}
11 }
```

On line 1, you'd provide your function's name in place of <name>. Function names should take the same form as a PowerShell cmdlet name: Verb-Noun, with the noun always being singular. Consider adding a unique prefix to your noun, so that it won't overlap with commands and functions that you may acquire from other people.

Lines 4 and 5 show a template for declaring an input parameter for the function. Always specify the <type> of data the parameter accepts, such as [string] or [int], and give the parameter a name. Try to use names that are consistent with the parameter names used by existing PowerShell cmdlets. For example, if a parameter will accept computer names, then $computerName is a good parameter name, since that's the name most cmdlets use for that purpose.

The bulk of the function occurs inside the BEGIN, PROCESS and END blocks. These are important elements – and are grossly misunderstood by most people. Here are some notes:

- Any of the three blocks can be omitted if you don't need to put any commands into them. Or, you can include them as empty blocks, as I've done in the template.

- If objects are piped to the function, then the BEGIN block will run first, and one time only. Then, PROCESS will execute one time for each object that was piped in. Finally, END will execute once.

- If nothing is piped into the function, and input is instead specified only via parameters, then BEGIN and END will never execute, and PROCESS will execute only once.

- BEGIN, PROCESS, and END all live within the same scope: the function's scope. These blocks do not create their own scope, so any variable created in any of the three blocks can be seen by all three. Similarly, you could create child functions within any of these three blocks, and they would be accessible to all three.

Those second two points really form the basis of advanced functions' difficulties. Because an advanced function might be run with pipeline input or without pipeline input, you can't predict in advance exactly how the function will execute. That's something we'll have to deal with, and it will be the biggest thing discussed in this chapter.

Designing the Function

Before I sit down to write a new function, I have to think about what I want it to do, and how I want it to work. I find that the best way for me to do that is to write some examples of how I want to use the function.

For this exercise, we'll to create a function called Get-DJOSInfo. The goal is to retrieve operating system (OS) information from one or more remote computers; I've included DJ as part of the function name so that it's less likely to overlap with other command names. That way, if my friend Jason writes a Get-OSInfo function, I can have both loaded into the shell at the same time, without conflict, because they have different names.

I'm going to have the function retrieve information from three different WMI classes:

- From the Win32_OperatingSystem class, I want the Caption, BuildNumber, OSArchitecture and ServicePackMajorVersion properties. However, OSArchitecture is normally a string, like "64-bit". I want to modify that in my output so that it's either 64 or 32, without the "-bit" part.

- From the Win32_BIOS class, I want the SerialNumber property.

- From the Win32_Processor class, I want the AddressWidth property. However, I only need this from the first processor in the system, since they're all the same.

I want to be able to retrieve this information from one or more computers, so I'll need a -computerName parameter that can accept one or more values. I'd like that parameter to be able to accept string values from the pipeline. I'd also like to be able to pipe in objects having a ComputerName property, and get that property's contents to feed my parameter – this is called pipeline binding ByPropertyName.

I'm not sure how I plan to feed computer names to the function, but that's okay. If I code this correctly, it will be able to work with an almost infinite variety of sources. However, I do want to add a -nameLog parameter, which would be a switch that doesn't accept any values. If specified, then the computer names I specify should be logged to a text file as the computers are contacted. That way, if something interrupts the function, I'll have a list of the computers that have already been attempted. If I don't specify that parameter, then no file should be created. I want the function to tack on a "-1," "-2" and so forth to the filename. So if the base filename is "names," then the first time should create "names-1.txt," the second time would create "names-2.txt" and so forth. I'll hardcode the base filename, rather than allowing it to be specified on a parameter.

That means I could potentially run this function in quite a few ways.

Usage Examples

```
01 # input from a text file via pipeline
02 Get-Content names.txt | Get-DSOSInfo
03
04 # input from a text file via parameter
05 Get-DJOSInfo -comp (Get-Content names.txt)
06
07 # just one, via parameter
08 Get-DJOSInfo -comp SERVER -nameLog
09
10 # names from AD, via pipeline
11 Import-Module ActiveDirectory
12 Get-ADComputer -filter * |
13 Select @{n='computername';e={$_.name}} |
14 Get-DJOSInfo -nameLog
15
16 # names from AD, via parameter
17 Get-DJOSInfo -comp (
18  Get-ADComputer -filter * |
19  Select -expand name
20 ) -nameLog
21
22 # just one, via pipeline
23 'localhost' | Get-DJOSInfo
```

I want to call special attention to that last one, on line 23. Notice that I didn't simply do this:

```
01 localhost | Get-DJOSInfo
```

You see, without the quotation marks around 'localhost,' PowerShell will think it's the name of a command, and attempt to execute it. Since there's no command named 'localhost,' I'd get an error. By wrapping the work in quotation marks, I'm explicitly telling PowerShell that it's a string, so the command works. Contrast that with line 8, where I didn't need to use the quotes. That's because, when passing a value to a parameter, PowerShell assumes that pretty much everything is a string, which saves you from always having to type quotation marks. If I actually had a command named "SERVER" that I wanted to run, I'd have to put it in parentheses. Doing so would force PowerShell to evaluate the contents of the parentheses from a fresh perspective.

Anyway, at this point I have the design for my function. I know what I want it to do, and I know how I want to use it.

Declaring Parameters

The next thing I'll do is declare the parameters. These provide the implementation for how I want my function to accept input. By doing this part first, I lock myself into my design.

Think about it this way: A function is supposed to be a black box. You've no idea what's happening inside. All you deal with are the buttons and gauges on the outside of the black box. I've already decided that I want a "computer name" dial and a "name log" button; declaring parameters actually creates those input controls.

Here's how it's done:

Listing 2-2: Declaring Parameters

```
01 function Get-DJOSInfo {
02   [CmdletBinding()]
03   param (
04     [Parameter(Mandatory=$True,
05         ValueFromPipeline=$True,
06         ValueFromPipelineByPropertyName=$True)]
07     [string[]]$computerName,
08
09     [Parameter()]
10     [switch]$nameLog
11   )
12   BEGIN {}
13   PROCESS {}
```

```
14   END {}
15 }
```

Make sure you're clear on why this is the right way to declare these parameters. The second one is the simplest, because its [Parameter()] attribute doesn't actually contain any instructions. It doesn't technically need to, since it's just a simple switch that the user will either specify or omit. The [Parameter()] bit is part of the parameter; I've typed it on a separate line just to keep things neat. I could have done this:

Alternate Parameter Formatting

```
01 [Parameter()][switch]$nameLog
```

That's still completely legal. The first parameter, $computerName, is the complicated one, because its [Parameter()] attribute includes three instructions. Those serve to make the parameter mandatory, permit it to accept pipeline input ByValue, and permit it to accept pipeline input ByPropertyName. If you're not familiar with those two pipeline input techniques, you should definitely review them before proceeding; they're covered very well in Learn Windows PowerShell in a Month of Lunches, which offers that and other beginner-level information.

So my parameters are officially declared. Now we can start using them.

Testing the Parameters

Before I even start writing any additional code, I want to make sure that my parameters are working correctly. To do this, I'll just add a tiny bit of code to output the state and content of the parameters, and then run my function with a couple of test calls.

I'm making use of the Write-Debug cmdlet to test my parameters. Normally, this cmdlet wouldn't produce any output, due to the setting of the shell's $DebugPreference variable. However, by using [CmdletBinding()] on my function, I get a little help from PowerShell. It automatically implements a -Debug parameter for me, with no work at all on my part. Using that parameter will turn on Write-Debug's output for the duration of my function. The Write-Debug cmdlet has an interesting side effect: It will pause your script. What that looks like differs a bit between the console, the ISE and third-party editors. For right now, I want that behavior. Later, we'll switch to something else to avoid the interruptions.

Listing 2-3: Parameter Test

```
01 function Get-DJOSInfo {
02   [CmdletBinding()]
03   param (
04     [Parameter(Mandatory=$True,
05         ValueFromPipeline=$True,
```

```
06          ValueFromPipelineByPropertyName=$True)]
07      [string[]]$computerName,
08
09      [Parameter()]
10      [switch]$nameLog
11   )
12   BEGIN {}
13   PROCESS {
14     if ($nameLog) {
15       Write-Debug 'Name logging on'
16     } else {
17       Write-Debug 'Name logging off'
18     }
19     Write-Debug "computer: $computerName"
20   }
21   END {}
22 }
23
24 Write-Host '----- TEST 1 -----'
25 'test1','test2' | Get-DJOSInfo -Debug
26
27 Write-Host '----- TEST 2 -----'
28 Get-DJOSInfo -comp 'test1','test2' -name -debug
```

Try running that complete script. (To do so, click the Run button in the PowerShell ISE toolbar – it looks like a green triangle; if you're not using the ISE, your editor should offer some kind of 'Run' button.) You probably won't like the results. The first test will go fine: You should see four lines of "DEBUG" output. Because I piped in two objects, the PROCESS block of the function executed two times. Each time through, $computerName contained a single computer name. Also note that my switch parameter, $nameLog, always contains True or False. Because it's declared as a [switch], PowerShell will make sure it always contains one of those two Boolean values. If the function is run without -nameLog, then $nameLog will contain False; otherwise, it will be True.

The second test, however, won't work so well. That's because I didn't pipe anything to the function, and so PROCESS executed only once, and $computerName contained an array of both computer names. This is the complexity I hinted at earlier: Writing a function that deals with both input scenarios is a pain in the neck.

Because it's possible for $computerName to contain more than one thing within a single execution of the PROCESS block, I have to enumerate its contents using a ForEach loop. This will be redundant in situations where I'm getting pipeline input, but necessary in cases where multiple values are coming directly on the parameter – as in the second test.

Listing 2-4: Fixing the Parameter Test

```
01 function Get-DJOSInfo {
02   [CmdletBinding()]
03   param (
```

```
04      [Parameter(Mandatory=$True,
05          ValueFromPipeline=$True,
06          ValueFromPipelineByPropertyName=$True)]
07      [string[]]$computerName,
08
09      [Parameter()]
10      [switch]$nameLog
11    )
12    BEGIN {}
13    PROCESS {
14      if ($nameLog) {
15        Write-Debug 'Name logging on'
16      } else {
17        Write-Debug 'Name logging off'
18      }
19      foreach ($computer in $computerName) {
20        Write-Debug "computer: $computer"
21      }
22    }
23    END {}
24 }
25
26 Write-Host '----- TEST 1 -----'
27 'test1','test2' | Get-DJOSInfo -Debug
28
29 Write-Host '----- TEST 2 -----'
30 Get-DJOSInfo -comp 'test1','test2' -name -debug
```

With this revision, my function works. Within the ForEach block, I'm guaranteed to have only a single computer name in the $computer variable, regardless of how the function was called. I'll leave the debugging code in place – it may come in handy later.

I find, however, that people can get really lost with the ForEach loop, so let's briefly review what's going on:

- In the event nothing is passed in via the pipeline, then the $computername parameter may contain 1 or more values, that I have to manually enumerate. That's what ForEach does.

- In the event that values are piped in, then $computername will only contain one value at a time, because the PROCESS block will implicitly enumerate them for me. The ForEach is redundant, but it doesn't slow things down.

Writing the Main Code

Now let's start putting some real code into the function. I'll do this in two stages, putting the main output-generating code in place first, and then adding the name logging functionality. Why not do it all at once? I like to go in baby steps, so that if I make mistakes, I can correct them as I go, rather than build upon them.

I'll be making WMI calls first, and those commands can become lengthy. If you're typing the script, remember that each numbered line is meant to be typed as a single line in your script editor.

Listing 2-5: Adding Functionality

```
01 function Get-DJOSInfo {
02   [CmdletBinding()]
03   param (
04     [Parameter(Mandatory=$True,
05         ValueFromPipeline=$True,
06         ValueFromPipelineByPropertyName=$True)]
07     [string[]]$computerName,
08
09     [Parameter()]
10     [switch]$nameLog
11   )
12   BEGIN {}
13   PROCESS {
14     Write-Verbose "Starting PROCESS block"
15     if ($nameLog) {
16       Write-Debug 'Name logging on'
17     } else {
18       Write-Debug 'Name logging off'
19     }
20     foreach ($computer in $computerName) {
21       Write-Debug "computer: $computer"
22       Write-Verbose "Querying WMI on $computer"
23       $os = Get-WmiObject -computerName $computer -class
   Win32_OperatingSystem
24       $bios = Get-WmiObject -computerName $computer -class Win32_BIOS
25       $proc = Get-WmiObject -computerName $computer -class
   Win32_Processor | Select-Object -first 1
26       $data = @{
27         'ComputerName'=$computer;
28         'SPVersion'=$os.servicepackmajorversion;
29         'OSName'=$os.caption;
30         'OSArchitecture'=$os.osarchitecture;
31         'OSBuild'=$os.buildnumber;
32         'ProcArchitecture'=$proc.addresswidth;
33         'BIOSSerial'=$bios.serialnumber
34       }
35       Write-Output (
36         New-Object -Type PSObject -Prop $data
37       )
38     }
39   }
40   END {}
41 }
42
43 Write-Host '----- TEST 1 -----'
44 'localhost','localhost' | Get-DJOSInfo -Verbose
45
46 Write-Host '----- TEST 2 -----'
47 Get-DJOSInfo -comp 'localhost','localhost' -name -Verbose
```

I've added some use of `Write-Verbose`. This works just like `Write-Debug`, except it's wired up to the automatically created -Verbose switch, instead of -Debug. There's no hard-and-fast line about when to use Verbose versus Debug. I kind of separate the two like this: If it's programmer-y stuff that I'm using to check my work, then I use `Write-Debug`. If it's step-by-step progress output, and I've taken the time to type everything neatly so that it's fit for human consumption, then I use `Write-Verbose`. You can make up your own rules about which to use. Of course, keep in mind that `Write-Debug` does that pausing thing – so you'll also have to decide if you want that feature or not.

I've used real computer names ("localhost") in my two test calls. Localhost will always work, so I don't have to worry about extraneous issues like network connectivity or permissions breaking things – I can just focus on my commands.

The syntax I've used to create an output object is the syntax I've come to prefer: Creating a hash table that contains property names and values, and then passing those to `New-Object` to create and populate the object all at once. Here's an alternate syntax for just a couple of properties that accomplishes the same thing:

Alternate Custom Object Syntax

```
01 $obj = New-Object -type PSObject
02 $obj | Add-Member -MemberType NoteProperty -Name Computername -Value
   $computer
03 $obj | Add-Member -MemberType NoteProperty -Name SPVersion -Value
   $os.servicepackmajorversion
```

You can see where that's headed, I hope, without me typing out all the properties used in the main example: You add more calls to `Add-Member`, one per property that you want to create. There's nothing technically wrong with this syntax, but it takes up a lot more room and may be more difficult to read in the long run. I like using it for beginners because it's perhaps clearer what's happening. But you're not a beginner anymore, so it's a good time to graduate to the more concise syntax.

Here's a variation to that alternate syntax, which relies on the -passThru parameter of `Add-Member`:

Alternate Custom Object Syntax

```
01 $obj = New-Object -type PSObject
02 $obj |
03 Add-Member -MemberType NoteProperty -Name Computername -Value
   $computer -passThru |
04 Add-Member -MemberType NoteProperty -Name SPVersion -Value
   $os.servicepackmajorversion
```

Again, you'll hopefully see where I'm going with that, without me having to add all of the properties that the real function is adding. Really, this is just appending all of the Add-Member commands together into a single logical pipeline. I don't think this is as human-readable, and still prefer the approach I used in Listing 2-5.

Outputting Custom Objects

An important lesson that I want to make sure to emphasize is this: Functions (and scripts) should output objects, not text. Never use Write-Output (or its alias, Write) or Write-Host to output text. Ever. Output objects, and let PowerShell format those objects, export them, filter them, sort them or whatever else needs to be done. One of the snarky "PowerShell Proverbs" I frequently use is this: "Every time you create a command that outputs text, God kills a puppy." Harsh, but it serves to convey the seriousness of the crime. Outputting text renders most of PowerShell's capabilities useless; outputting objects lets PowerShell do a great deal of heavy lifting for a huge variety of tasks.

If this whole "object" and "custom object output" thing is confusing, then let's just change the terminology a bit to make it clearer.

The reason PowerShell works the way it does is because cmdlets (and functions) both output, and accept as input, a specific type of data structure. That structure is not at all unlike a table, or an Excel spreadsheet. In fact, run Get-Process and you basically see a truncated example of what that data structure looks like. Because each column has a name, PowerShell is easily able to pick apart just pieces of the data – grabbing just the columns you want, or just the rows with particular values in particular columns. By building your own functions' output in this kind of tabular data structure, you enable your output to interact with all the other PowerShell commands.

Now, just change "table" to "collection," change "row" to "object," and change "column" to "property," and you'll be on the right page with PowerShell's own terminology. A cmdlet (or function) produces a collection of objects, and those objects each have an identical set of properties. Actually, those objects also have other things like methods and events, which we tend not to use often in PowerShell. Collectively, the properties, methods, and events are called "members," and that's why you pipe objects to Get-Member to see a list of those things.

Continuing With the Advanced Function

Give Listing 2-5 a run and it'll work – but it isn't exactly what I wanted. Notice the contents of the OSArchitecture property in the output? I said I wanted a simple "64" or "32," but that's not what I'm getting. Time for a revision.

Listing 2-6: Fixing the Output

```
01 function Get-DJOSInfo {
02   [CmdletBinding()]
03   param (
04     [Parameter(Mandatory=$True,
05         ValueFromPipeline=$True,
06         ValueFromPipelineByPropertyName=$True)]
07     [string[]]$computerName,
08
09     [Parameter()]
10     [switch]$nameLog
11   )
12   BEGIN {}
13   PROCESS {
14     Write-Verbose "Starting PROCESS block"
15     if ($nameLog) {
16       Write-Debug 'Name logging on'
17     } else {
18       Write-Debug 'Name logging off'
19     }
20     foreach ($computer in $computerName) {
21       Write-Debug "computer: $computer"
22       Write-Verbose "Querying WMI on $computer"
23       $os = Get-WmiObject -computerName $computer -class
   Win32_OperatingSystem
24       $bios = Get-WmiObject -computerName $computer -class Win32_BIOS
25       $proc = Get-WmiObject -computerName $computer -class
   Win32_Processor | Select-Object -first 1
26       if ($os.osarchitecture -like '*64*') {
27         $osarch = 64
28       } else {
29         $osarch = 32
30       }
31       $data = @{
32         'ComputerName'=$computer;
33         'SPVersion'=$os.servicepackmajorversion;
34         'OSName'=$os.caption;
35         'OSArchitecture'=$osarch;
36         'OSBuild'=$os.buildnumber;
37         'ProcArchitecture'=$proc.addresswidth;
38         'BIOSSerial'=$bios.serialnumber
39       }
40       Write-Output (
41         New-Object -Type PSObject -Prop $data
42       )
43     }
44   }
45   END {}
46 }
47
48 Write-Host '----- TEST 1 -----'
49 'localhost','localhost' | Get-DJOSInfo -Verbose
50
```

```
51 Write-Host '----- TEST 2 -----'
52 Get-DJOSInfo -comp localhost -verbose
```

That should do it. Now, I can go about adding my name logging feature. This will be a bit tricky. At the start of my function, I need to find a free filename - "name-1.txt", "name-2.txt" and so on. Here's the approach I take.

Listing 2-7: Adding the Logging

```
01 function Get-DJOSInfo {
02      [CmdletBinding()]
03      param (
04      [Parameter(Mandatory=$True,
05          ValueFromPipeline=$True,
06          ValueFromPipelineByPropertyName=$True)]
07      [string[]]$computerName,
08
09      [Parameter()]
10      [switch]$nameLog
11      )
12      BEGIN {
13          Write-Verbose 'Setting name log filename'
14          $i = 0
15          Do {
16          $i++
17          $logFile = "names-$i.txt"
18          Write-Verbose "Trying $logFile"
19          } While (Test-Path $logFile)
20          New-Variable -name nameLogFile -Value $logFile
21          Write-Verbose "Filename is $logFile"
22      }
23      PROCESS {
24      Write-Verbose "Starting PROCESS block"
25      if ($nameLog) {
26          Write-Debug 'Name logging on'
27      } else {
28          Write-Debug 'Name logging off'
29      }
30      foreach ($computer in $computerName) {
31          if ($nameLog) {
32          Write-Debug "Logging $computer to $nameLogFile"
33          $computer | Out-File $nameLogFile -append
34          }
35          Write-Debug "computer: $computer"
36          Write-Verbose "Querying WMI on $computer"
37          $os = Get-WmiObject -computerName $computer -class
   Win32_OperatingSystem
38          $bios = Get-WmiObject -computerName $computer -class
   Win32_BIOS
39          $proc = Get-WmiObject -computerName $computer -class
   Win32_Processor | Select-Object -first 1
40          if ($os.osarchitecture -like '*64*') {
41          $osarch = 64
42          } else {
43          $osarch = 32
```

```
44              }
45              $data = @{
46              'ComputerName'=$computer;
47              'SPVersion'=$os.servicepackmajorversion;
48              'OSName'=$os.caption;
49              'OSArchitecture'=$osarch;
50              'OSBuild'=$os.buildnumber;
51              'ProcArchitecture'=$proc.addresswidth;
52              'BIOSSerial'=$bios.serialnumber
53              }
54              Write-Output (
55              New-Object -Type PSOBject -Prop $data
56              )
57          }
58          }
59      END {}
60 }
61
62 Write-Host '----- TEST 1 -----'
63 'localhost','localhost' | Get-DJOSInfo -namelog -Verbose
64
65 Write-Host '----- TEST 2 -----'
66 Get-DJOSInfo -comp localhost,localhost -namelog -Verbose
```

Because there are two distinct ways in which this function might execute, let me walk you through each of them.

First, let's assume we're piping input to the function (which was Test 1). BEGIN will execute first, I look for an available variable name, incrementing a counter ($i) until I find a filename that doesn't already exist. Once I find one, I copy that filename into the $nameLogFile variable.

Next, the PROCESS block will begin executing. It will see that the $SetupDone variable already exists, so it won't call Setup again. You can see where I'm writing the contents of $computer to that $nameLogFile filename.

Second, consider the case where nothing is piped in (that's what Test 2 did). The execution process is essentially the same: BEGIN first, PROCESS just once, and then END (which is empty). Because PROCESS only executes once, I have to manually "unwind" the $computername variable, which my foreach loop takes care of.

Try running this, and consider adding -Debug to the two test calls so that you can see the additional output I've added. It's perfectly fine to have both -Debug and -Verbose at the same time.

Make sure you understand the logic that's happening within this function. In fact, I suggest taking a pencil and a piece of paper and walking through this functioning your head. Make a note of what each variable contains as you "run" the function mentally. Make a note of what output you expect to see. Then run the function again, and see if your expectations reflect what really happens. If the real output matches your expectations, then you're

good. If not, either fix the function or your expectations and do it again –
and keep doing that until it's right.

Testing the Function

Up to this point, we've been testing my new function by simply including
calls to it within the same script. That's not ideal, in part because the
PowerShell ISE doesn't maintain a distinct global scope, and in part
because running scripts in an editor isn't a real-world test of how the
script will be used on a regular basis. Ideally, I'd like to test the function in
the normal PowerShell console window, since that's the "gold standard"
for testing. If something works there, it should work anywhere.

Getting the function into the global shell is the problem. We can't just run
the script; doing so creates a scope, defines the function within that scope,
and then exits – discarding the scope and the function. Instead, we need to
run the script in the shell without creating a new scope. PowerShell
provides a technique called dot sourcing to accomplish that. It's far from
ideal – as you'll see in a moment – but for now it will suffice.

To begin with, let's remove the test lines from our script.

Listing 2-8: Final Function to Test

```
01 function Get-DJOSInfo {
02   [CmdletBinding()]
03   param (
04     [Parameter(Mandatory=$True,
05         ValueFromPipeline=$True,
06         ValueFromPipelineByPropertyName=$True)]
07     [string[]]$computerName,
08
09     [Parameter()]
10     [switch]$nameLog
11   )
12   BEGIN {
13     Write-Verbose 'Setting name log filename'
14     $i = 0
15     Do {
16       $i++
17       $logFile = "names-$i.txt"
18       Write-Verbose "Trying $logFile"
19     } While (Test-Path $logFile)
20     New-Variable -name nameLogFile -Value $logFile
21     Write-Verbose "Filename is $logFile"
22   }
23   PROCESS {
24     Write-Verbose "Starting PROCESS block"
25     if ($nameLog) {
26       Write-Debug 'Name logging on'
27     } else {
28       Write-Debug 'Name logging off'
29     }
```

```
30    foreach ($computer in $computerName) {
31      if ($nameLog) {
32        Write-Debug "Logging $computer to $nameLogFile"
33        $computer | Out-File $nameLogFile -append
34      }
35      Write-Debug "computer: $computer"
36      Write-Verbose "Querying WMI on $computer"
37      $os = Get-WmiObject -computerName $computer -class
   Win32_OperatingSystem
38      $bios = Get-WmiObject -computerName $computer -class Win32_BIOS
39      $proc = Get-WmiObject -computerName $computer -class
   Win32_Processor | Select-Object -first 1
40      if ($os.osarchitecture -like '*64*') {
41        $osarch = 64
42      } else {
43        $osarch = 32
44      }
45      $data = @{
46        'ComputerName'=$computer;
47        'SPVersion'=$os.servicepackmajorversion;
48        'OSName'=$os.caption;
49        'OSArchitecture'=$osarch;
50        'OSBuild'=$os.buildnumber;
51        'ProcArchitecture'=$proc.addresswidth;
52        'BIOSSerial'=$bios.serialnumber
53      }
54      Write-Output (
55        New-Object -Type PSOBject -Prop $data
56      )
57    }
58  }
59  END {}
60 }
```

Save that someplace easy to get to, like C:\Scripts\Tools.ps1. Then, go into the console window and dot-source it. I'll point out that I'm assuming the filename is Tools.ps1; if you're using the downloaded versions of these scripts, then the above will have a filename like "Listing2-8.ps1." That's fine: Simply copy the file to C:\Scripts\Tools.ps1 if you want to follow along. You'll need to do that for each successive new version of the script.

Dot-Sourcing the Script

```
01 . C:\Scripts\Tools.ps1
```

The space after the first dot is crucial – without it, this command won't work properly. Once you've run it, you should be able to look at a directory listing of the FUNCTION: drive and see the Get-DJOSInfo function. You should also be able to run Get-DJOSInfo simply by typing its name – or, better yet, by typing Get-DJO and pressing Tab to complete the name. Try it.

A problem with this dot-sourcing technique is that the function isn't associated with the script anymore – it's just defined within the shell's global scope. We can't easily remove every function that was defined in that script. For now, of course, there's only one function – so if we want to remove it, we could just run Del FUNCTION:\Get-DJOSInfo and it would be gone. We'll need to do that if we make changes to the function and want to re-load it into the shell.

There's a better technique for packaging, loading and unloading a script full of functions, but we'll come to that later. For now, dot-sourcing will do. Through the next few chapters, you'll see successive iterations of this Get-DJOSInfo function; for each one, you have a choice. You can either delete the function and re-dot-source it, or you can simply close the shell, open a new shell window, and dot-source the revised script. Your choice.

To Remove and Re-Load the Function

```
01 Del FUNCTION:\Get-DJOSInfo
02 . <path>\<filename>.ps1
```

Conclusion

This chapter has covered the very basics of PowerShell advanced functions. You'll spend a lot more time with these in upcoming chapters. In fact, the Get-DJOSInfo function is one we'll continue to build on, adding functionality and capabilities. Our tools.ps1 script will eventually have additional functions added as well, making it into a true "utility belt" of tools that we can share and use whenever we like.

Advanced Functions, Advanced

In this chapter, we'll build on the Get-DJOSInfo function, adding more functionality to it. I'll admit up front that some of the things we'll do might not seem particularly real-world – but they'll serve as excellent examples of how to accomplish specific goals, so that when you need to use these tricks in the real world you'll have something to refer back to.

Testing, Testing, Testing

First of all, you're going to be testing this function a lot. That means you'll need to remove it and re-load it a lot. You might want to simplify that process. Just type these next few lines of code directly into the PowerShell console window. If you're using a profile script, type them into your profile.

Listing 3-1: Function Reloader

```
01 function Relo {
02   param($filename)
03   Del FUNCTION:\Get-DJOSInfo
04   copy $filename c:\scripts\tools.ps1 -force
05   . C:\Scripts\Tools.ps1
06 }
07
```

If you typed that directly into the shell, hit Enter on the final, blank line to save the function.

Now, whenever you want to un-load and re-load the function, just run Relo within the shell. This isn't a fancy function: Both the function name it removes, and the script it loads, are hardcoded. This is really just to save you a bit of typing down the line. When you run Relo, give it the filename that you want to use from the downloaded sample scripts. For example, to reload the Get-DJOSInfo function from the Listing7-2.ps1 file:

Using the Function Reloader

```
01 Relo c:\samples\listing7-2.ps1
```

That assumes you've downloaded your sample scripts to C:\Samples, of course.

Honestly, by the end of Chapter 7 you won't even need this anymore, since we'll find a better way to package this function so that it can be managed more easily and consistently.

Verbose and Debug Output

In the previous chapter, I'd already gotten a start on verbose and debug output by using Write-Debug and Write-Verbose. I explained that Write-Debug, for me, is a way to display "internal" information from the script, such as the contents of specific variables, so that I can verify what's happening if I need to debug the script. Verbose information, for me, is more formal output that I'd expect the function's user to sometimes want to see. Part of the distinction is also the fact that using the -Debug parameter makes the script pause each time debug output is displayed, so my Debug output is usually directly related to my debugging procedures.

I also rely on debug and verbose output to serve as inline comments within the script, to help document what it's doing. For me, these replace the more traditional programmer-style comments (which PowerShell does support). Best yet, by using the -Verbose and -Debug switches, these "comments" can prove useful to someone running the script as well as someone reading it.

As you saw in the previous chapter, I tend to start throwing in Write-Verbose and Write-Debug calls as I write a function. However, it's always a good idea to go back after you're done and make sure you've documented everything as thoroughly as possible. My guidelines:

- If I'm going to rely on the contents of a variable, I output those contents so that I can check them as the script runs.

- If I'm going to make a decision – such as using an If construct – I want to see output no matter which way the decision goes.

- I want output prior to any long-running task, like connecting to a remote computer. This helps give the person running the script some "warm and fuzzy" if they use the -Verbose switch, just to let them know everything's okay.

There's also Write-Progress, which displays a nicely formatted progress bar and status information for long-running tasks. Right now, our function isn't doing anything long-running apart from waiting on WMI, so I'm not going to dive into Write-Progress. However, it's there in case you need it – and you can read the cmdlet's help for examples on how to use it.

For now, let's get some more verbose and debug output into our running example. Don't forget: You'll have to delete the old Get-DJOSInfo function and dot-source this new script into the console so that you can test it. Refer to the last part of the previous chapter for more information on that, or use the Relo function from the first part of this chapter. For example, if the below script is in C:\Scripts\Listing3-2.ps1, you could run Relo C:\Scripts\Listing3-2.ps1 to get this new version of Get-DJOSInfo into the shell for testing. Then, run something like Get-DJOSInfo -namelog -computername localhost,localhost -verbose -debug or `'localhost','localhost' | Get-DJOSInfo -verbose -debug` to test the new version of the function.

Did you Notice?
Have you noticed that I enclose 'localhost' in quotes when I'm piping it, but I don't when I'm passing it to a parameter? If I just ran `localhost | Get-DJOSInfo`, I'd get an error, because the shell would look for a command called localhost – and there isn't one. I have to use the quotes to force the shell to recognize the string. Quotes will work the other way, too: `Get-DJOSInfo -computername 'localhost'` but they aren't necessary, because the shell assumes that parameter's values are strings when the parameter itself is declared as a [string].

Listing 3-2: Adding Verbose and Debug Output

```
01 function Get-DJOSInfo {
02   [CmdletBinding()]
03   param (
04     [Parameter(Mandatory=$True,
05         ValueFromPipeline=$True,
06         ValueFromPipelineByPropertyName=$True)]
07     [string[]]$computerName,
08
09     [Parameter()]
10     [switch]$nameLog
11   )
12   BEGIN {
13     Write-Verbose 'Setting name log filename'
14     $i = 0
15     Do {
16       $i++
17       $logFile = "names-$i.txt"
18       Write-Verbose "Trying $logFile"
19     } While (Test-Path $logFile)
20     New-Variable -name nameLogFile -Value $logFile
21     Write-Verbose "Filename is $logFile"
22   }
23   PROCESS {
24     Write-Verbose "Starting PROCESS block"
25     if ($nameLog) {
26       Write-Debug 'Name logging on'
27     } else {
28       Write-Debug 'Name logging off'
29     }
30     foreach ($computer in $computerName) {
31       if ($nameLog) {
32         Write-Debug "Logging $computer to $nameLogFile"
33         $computer | Out-File $nameLogFile -append
34       }
35       Write-Debug "computer: $computer"
```

```
36        Write-Verbose "Querying WMI on $computer (step 1)"
37        $os = Get-WmiObject -computerName $computer -class
   Win32_OperatingSystem
38        Write-Verbose "Querying WMI on $computer (step 2)"
39        $bios = Get-WmiObject -computerName $computer -class Win32_BIOS
40        Write-Verbose "Querying WMI on $computer (step 3)"
41        $proc = Get-WmiObject -computerName $computer -class
   Win32_Processor | Select-Object -first 1
42        if ($os.osarchitecture -like '*64*') {
43           $osarch = 64
44               Write-Debug "OS Architecture 64 bit"
45        } else {
46               Write-Debug "OS Architecture 32 bit"
47           $osarch = 32
48        }
49        $data = @{
50           'ComputerName'=$computer;
51           'SPVersion'=$os.servicepackmajorversion;
52           'OSName'=$os.caption;
53           'OSArchitecture'=$osarch;
54           'OSBuild'=$os.buildnumber;
55           'ProcArchitecture'=$proc.addresswidth;
56           'BIOSSerial'=$bios.serialnumber
57        }
58         Write-Verbose 'Writing output to pipeline'
59         Write-Output (
60            New-Object -Type PSObject -Prop $data
61         )
62      }
63    }
64   END {}
65 }
```

Parameter Aliases

In my function, I've used the -computerName parameter to accept one or more computer names. The choice of "computerName" for the parameter was deliberate: Every native PowerShell cmdlet that needs a computer name accepts it on a -computerName parameter. So by choosing that name, I'm being consistent with the rest of the shell.

A problem, however, is that not everyone who uses my function might expect that parameter name. Perhaps they're used to an older in-house utility that had a -host or -hostname switch. A parameter alias would let me continue using the PowerShell-consistent -computerName parameter, while also allowing the use of -host or -hostname. The alias, -hostname, won't show up in the function's generated help or anywhere else. It will just be there for a user who is expecting it, and who tries to use it without bothering to read the help.

You've probably already run into parameter aliases without realizing it. Invoke-Command permits you to type -command in place of -scriptBlock, and

Get-Command accepts -pssnapin in place of -module. Those are parameter aliases.

Here's how to make one:

Listing 3-3: Adding a Parameter Alias

```
01 function Get-DJOSInfo {
02   [CmdletBinding()]
03   param (
04     [Parameter(Mandatory=$True,
05         ValueFromPipeline=$True,
06         ValueFromPipelineByPropertyName=$True)]
07       [Alias('host')]
08     [string[]]$computerName,
09
10     [Parameter()]
11     [switch]$nameLog
12   )
13   BEGIN {
14     Write-Verbose 'Setting name log filename'
15     $i = 0
16     Do {
17       $i++
18       $logFile = "names-$i.txt"
19       Write-Verbose "Trying $logFile"
20     } While (Test-Path $logFile)
21     New-Variable -name nameLogFile -Value $logFile
22     Write-Verbose "Filename is $logFile"
23   }
24   PROCESS {
25     Write-Verbose "Starting PROCESS block"
26     if ($nameLog) {
27       Write-Debug 'Name logging on'
28     } else {
29       Write-Debug 'Name logging off'
30     }
31     foreach ($computer in $computerName) {
32       if ($nameLog) {
33         Write-Debug "Logging $computer to $nameLogFile"
34         $computer | Out-File $nameLogFile -append
35       }
36       Write-Debug "computer: $computer"
37       Write-Verbose "Querying WMI on $computer (step 1)"
38       $os = Get-WmiObject -computerName $computer -class
   Win32_OperatingSystem
39       Write-Verbose "Querying WMI on $computer (step 2)"
40       $bios = Get-WmiObject -computerName $computer -class Win32_BIOS
41       Write-Verbose "Querying WMI on $computer (step 3)"
42       $proc = Get-WmiObject -computerName $computer -class
   Win32_Processor | Select-Object -first 1
43       if ($os.osarchitecture -like '*64*') {
44         $osarch = 64
45             Write-Debug "OS Architecture 64 bit"
46       } else {
47             Write-Debug "OS Architecture 32 bit"
48         $osarch = 32
```

```
49        }
50        $data = @{
51          'ComputerName'=$computer;
52          'SPVersion'=$os.servicepackmajorversion;
53          'OSName'=$os.caption;
54          'OSArchitecture'=$osarch;
55          'OSBuild'=$os.buildnumber;
56          'ProcArchitecture'=$proc.addresswidth;
57          'BIOSSerial'=$bios.serialnumber
58        }
59          Write-Verbose 'Writing output to pipeline'
60        Write-Output (
61          New-Object -Type PSObject -Prop $data
62        )
63      }
64    }
65    END {}
66 }
```

Parameter Validation

PowerShell can do an awful lot of heavy lifting for your functions, if you let it. For example, one thing you may need to do in some functions is check the input that you've been given before using that input. You might validate a computer name, check an input range and so on. PowerShell can actually do all that for you, before your code even runs.

Now, this is the section with examples that aren't entirely real-world applicable. For that reason, I'll stick mainly with partial examples, just so you can see the syntax and have something to refer back to. For the final example, I'll actually add something to the Get-DJOSInfo function, so you've got something you can test directly.

Like everything else we've been doing thus far with function parameters, validation takes the form of an attribute on the parameter itself. For the first example, let's say that you have a parameter that accepts a UNC path. You want the input to be a three-part path: \\Server\Share\Folder. One way to validate that is to use a regular expression. This won't validate that the UNC path is legal, but it will validate that the input looks like a properly formatted path.

Validate Using RegEx

```
01 param(
02   [Parameter(Mandatory=$True)]
03   [ValidatePattern('^\\\\\w+\\\w+\\\w+$')]
04   [string]$uncPath
05 )
```

In another example, suppose you have a parameter that will accept the last octet of an IPv4 address. Legal addresses in your company might not include the full 1-255 range that's technically possible, and you might want to restrict the input to the function to just the valid range. Let's say your network subnets only have hosts ranging from 2 to 100.

Validating a Range

```
01 param(
02    [Parameter(ValueFromPipeline=$True)]
03    [ValidateRange(2,100)]
04    [int]$lastOctet
05 )
```

Notice in these examples that I always start with the [Parameter()] attribute, and just for illustration I'm using some of the valid items within that, such as Mandatory and ValueFromPipeline. You can still use the [Validatexxxxxx()] attributes even if [Parameter()] is completely empty.

If you've created a parameter that accepts multiple values, you might want to restrict how many values are passed in. For example, let's say we want a -computerName parameter to accept multiple names, but we don't want to accept more than ten at a time.

Validating Item Count

```
01 param(
02    [Parameter()]
03    [ValidateCount(1,10)]
04    [string[]]$computerName
05 )
```

It's legal to have more than one [Validatexxxxxx()] attribute on a single parameter. PowerShell will only accept input that passes all of the provided validation checks. For example, let's say that in our environment, computer names are always 8 to 12 characters in length. We could have PowerShell check that for us.

Validating Item Length

```
01 param(
02    [Parameter()]
03    [ValidateCount(1,10)]
04    [ValidateLength(8,12)]
05    [string[]]$computerName
06 )
```

Another example might be only accepting specific values. Suppose I've created a function that will restart a computer, power it off and so forth. I want to provide an -action parameter that tells the function exactly what to do, but I only want to accept certain values: LogOff, PowerOff, Shutdown, and Restart.

Validating a Set of Values

```
01 param(
```

```
02   [Parameter()]
03   [ValidateSet('LogOff','PowerOff',
04                'Shutdown','Restart')]
05   [string]$action
06 )
```

Finally, when all else fails, you can actually write a little mini-script, which PowerShell will execute, to perform validation. This is the right thing to do when none of the built-in validation mechanisms are suitable for your needs. You'll provide a complete script for this, and it must return either $True or $False at its end. To access the value that the user provided to the parameter, use the special $_ placeholder. Here's a quick example, which checks to see if a provided date is in the future.

Validating with a Script

```
01 param(
02   [Parameter(Mandatory=$True)]
03   [ValidateScript({
04     $_ -ge (Get-Date)
05   })]
06   [date]$scheduleDate
07 )
```

For the last two validation techniques, a bit of background explanation is needed. PowerShell maintains a distinction between an empty collection – that is, a box with no items in it – and the special value Null, which the shell represents as $null. While not always helpful, $null is a real value, and so it's possible for someone to "bypass" a mandatory parameter by passing $null instead of something more useful. You can stop that with a validation attribute.

Validating Not Null

```
01 param(
02   [Parameter(Mandatory=$True)]
03   [ValidateNotNull()]
04   [string]$data
05 )
```

Finally, you can also check to make sure a collection actually contains items, rather than just being an "empty box." This is where we'll bring Get-DJOSInfo back into play, by adding a validation attribute to its –computerName parameter.

Listing 3-4: Validating for a Non-Null, Non-Empty Collection

```
01 function Get-DJOSInfo {
02   [CmdletBinding()]
03   param (
04     [Parameter(Mandatory=$True,
05         ValueFromPipeline=$True,
06         ValueFromPipelineByPropertyName=$True)]
```

```
07        [Alias('host')]
08        [ValidateNotNullorEmpty()]
09      [string[]]$computerName,
10
11      [Parameter()]
12      [switch]$nameLog
13    )
14    BEGIN {
15      Write-Verbose 'Setting name log filename'
16      $i = 0
17      Do {
18        $i++
19        $logFile = "names-$i.txt"
20        Write-Verbose "Trying $logFile"
21      } While (Test-Path $logFile)
22      New-Variable -name nameLogFile -Value $logFile
23      Write-Verbose "Filename is $logFile"
24    }
25    PROCESS {
26      Write-Verbose "Starting PROCESS block"
27      if ($nameLog) {
28        Write-Debug 'Name logging on'
29      } else {
30        Write-Debug 'Name logging off'
31      }
32      foreach ($computer in $computerName) {
33        if ($nameLog) {
34          Write-Debug "Logging $computer to $nameLogFile"
35          $computer | Out-File $nameLogFile -append
36        }
37        Write-Debug "computer: $computer"
38        Write-Verbose "Querying WMI on $computer (step 1)"
39        $os = Get-WmiObject -computerName $computer -class
    Win32_OperatingSystem
40        Write-Verbose "Querying WMI on $computer (step 2)"
41        $bios = Get-WmiObject -computerName $computer -class Win32_BIOS
42        Write-Verbose "Querying WMI on $computer (step 3)"
43        $proc = Get-WmiObject -computerName $computer -class
    Win32_Processor | Select-Object -first 1
44        if ($os.osarchitecture -like '*64*') {
45          $osarch = 64
46              Write-Debug "OS Architecture 64 bit"
47        } else {
48              Write-Debug "OS Architecture 32 bit"
49          $osarch = 32
50        }
51        $data = @{
52          'ComputerName'=$computer;
53          'SPVersion'=$os.servicepackmajorversion;
54          'OSName'=$os.caption;
55          'OSArchitecture'=$osarch;
56          'OSBuild'=$os.buildnumber;
57          'ProcArchitecture'=$proc.addresswidth;
58          'BIOSSerial'=$bios.serialnumber
59        }
60        Write-Verbose 'Writing output to pipeline'
61        Write-Output (
```

```
62        New-Object -Type PSObject -Prop $data
63      )
64    }
65  }
66  END {}
67 }
```

Parameter Help

We've coded the Get-DJOSInfo function so that the -computerName parameter is mandatory. If someone tries to run the function without providing any input to that parameter – either directly, or through the pipeline – then the shell will prompt them to enter one or more computer names. It's actually neat how the shell does it: Because we declared the parameter as being of type [string[]], it knows that multiple values are acceptable. So it'll continue prompting for computer names until the user hits Enter on an empty prompt, telling the shell "that's all, go ahead and execute now."

A problem with our current function is that it isn't always clear what the shell is prompting for. We can fix that by providing a short description. The shell will display this when prompting. We can also add a brief help message to any other parameters, although the help message is most useful for mandatory parameters.

Listing 3-5: Adding Parameter Help

```
01 function Get-DJOSInfo {
02   [CmdletBinding()]
03   param (
04     [Parameter(Mandatory=$True,
05         ValueFromPipeline=$True,
06         ValueFromPipelineByPropertyName=$True,
07             HelpMessage='One or more computer names to query')]
08     [Alias('host')]
09     [ValidateNotNullorEmpty()]
10     [string[]]$computerName,
11
12     [Parameter(
13             HelpMessage='Write attempted computer names to a log')]
14     [switch]$nameLog
15   )
16   BEGIN {
17     Write-Verbose 'Setting name log filename'
18     $i = 0
19     Do {
20       $i++
21       $logFile = "names-$i.txt"
22       Write-Verbose "Trying $logFile"
23     } While (Test-Path $logFile)
24     New-Variable -name nameLogFile -Value $logFile
25     Write-Verbose "Filename is $logFile"
26   }
```

```
27  PROCESS {
28    Write-Verbose "Starting PROCESS block"
29    if ($nameLog) {
30      Write-Debug 'Name logging on'
31    } else {
32      Write-Debug 'Name logging off'
33    }
34    foreach ($computer in $computerName) {
35      if ($nameLog) {
36        Write-Debug "Logging $computer to $nameLogFile"
37        $computer | Out-File $nameLogFile -append
38      }
39      Write-Debug "computer: $computer"
40      Write-Verbose "Querying WMI on $computer (step 1)"
41      $os = Get-WmiObject -computerName $computer -class
   Win32_OperatingSystem
42      Write-Verbose "Querying WMI on $computer (step 2)"
43      $bios = Get-WmiObject -computerName $computer -class Win32_BIOS
44      Write-Verbose "Querying WMI on $computer (step 3)"
45      $proc = Get-WmiObject -computerName $computer -class
   Win32_Processor | Select-Object -first 1
46      if ($os.osarchitecture -like '*64*') {
47        $osarch = 64
48          Write-Debug "OS Architecture 64 bit"
49      } else {
50          Write-Debug "OS Architecture 32 bit"
51        $osarch = 32
52      }
53      $data = @{
54        'ComputerName'=$computer;
55        'SPVersion'=$os.servicepackmajorversion;
56        'OSName'=$os.caption;
57        'OSArchitecture'=$osarch;
58        'OSBuild'=$os.buildnumber;
59        'ProcArchitecture'=$proc.addresswidth;
60        'BIOSSerial'=$bios.serialnumber
61      }
62        Write-Verbose 'Writing output to pipeline'
63      Write-Output (
64        New-Object -Type PSObject -Prop $data
65      )
66    }
67  }
68  END {}
69 }
```

Parameter Sets

This is probably the hardest thing to do with a function that you write yourself, in part because a lot of people don't properly understand how PowerShell parameter sets operate.

Take a look at the help for Get-WmiObject. You'll notice several parameter sets – the blocks of syntax that are separated from each other by a blank line. Notice that one parameter set includes the -query parameter, while a couple of others include the -class parameter. Because those parameters are in different parameter sets, they can never be used together. You'll never see a valid Get-WmiObject command that includes both -query and -class because those two parameters don't exist in the same parameter set. There are certainly many parameters, such as –credential, which exist in multiple sets, and you can use them almost anytime you're running Get-WmiObject. But the parameters within a set are exclusive; once you decide to use -query, you can only use other parameters that appear within its same set.

You can define these same parameter sets when you create your own functions. For example, right now Get-DJOSInfo has a -computerName and a -nameLog parameter. The -computerName parameter accepts String objects, which we expect to be computer names or even IP addresses. What if we also wanted to be able to accept Active Directory computer objects, like the kind produced by the Windows Server 2008 R2 ActiveDirectory module? Perhaps a -computerObject parameter would be appropriate for that. We might want to use -nameLog along with that, so we'll need two parameter sets.

This can become tricky, because the body of the function itself must figure out which one was used, so that it knows which parameter to pull data from. Here's how it could be done.

Listing 3-6: Adding a Parameter Set

```
01   param (
02      [Parameter(Mandatory=$True,
03         ValueFromPipeline=$True,
04         ValueFromPipelineByPropertyName=$True,
05            HelpMessage='One or more computer names to query',
06            ParameterSetName='Names')]
07      [Alias('host')]
08      [ValidateNotNullorEmpty()]
09      [string[]]$computerName,
10
11      [Parameter(Mandatory=$true,
12            ValueFromPipeline=$True,
13            HelpMessage='One or more AD computer objects to query',
14            ParameterSetName='Computers')]
15
        [Microsoft.ActiveDirectory.Management.ADComputer[]]$computerObj
   ect,
16
17      [Parameter(
18            HelpMessage='Write attempted computer names to a log')]
19      [switch]$nameLog
20   )
```

Notice that I added an attribute to each parameter, telling PowerShell which set each one belongs to. The parameter set names are entirely made up for my own convenience; these will never be seen by a user of the function. The names are just there so that I have a convenient, human-readable way of grouping the parameters. Pay special attention to the -nameLog parameter, which appears in both parameter sets. See how I made that happen? You simply don't add it to any parameter set, making it appear in all of them. You do need to ensure that each parameter set has at least one unique parameter that does not appear in any other set.

I admit, I have misgivings about adding that -computerObject parameter. As I'll explain in the next section of this chapter, a function shouldn't worry about where its input is coming from. It would have been completely possible to use those AD computer objects with the original -computerName parameter, simply by doing some in-pipeline mangling of the objects. For example, this would have worked:

Custom Properties to Align Pipeline Input

```
01 Get-ADComputer -filter * |
02 Select @{n='computername';e={$_.name}} |
03 Get-DJOSInfo
```

We didn't really need to directly accept the computer objects. But having the two parameter sets is convenient because it eliminates the need to do that object manipulation in the pipeline. Plus, it's a good example of how to do multiple parameter sets!

There's a bit more work that has to be done when you're relying on multiple parameter sets like this. I would need to go into the PROCESS block of the function and test to see if $computername or $computerObject contained something, and then deal with each scenario appropriately. To keep the Get-DJOSInfo function a bit simpler for future examples, I won't include the -computerObject parameter going forward.

Designing Functions

As a final topic for this chapter, I want to touch briefly on the idea of function design. The goal with designing a function should be to make it work, as much as possible, like a native PowerShell cmdlet. That's what all of these parameter attributes have been about – giving your functions the ability to work just like "real" commands. In fact, when a VB or C# developer sits down with Visual Studio to author a real cmdlet, they're using many of the same options that we covered in this chapter, albeit with a somewhat different syntax.

The most important design feature of a real PowerShell cmdlet – and therefore, of your functions – is the idea of making them single-task. A cmdlet should do only one of these things:

- Retrieve data from someplace, probably with the idea of piping that data to another cmdlet

- Do something – execute some task, for example
- Save data to someplace, usually data that's been piped in from another cmdlet

You can see these same patterns in real PowerShell cmdlets. Get-Service does just that: Gets services. It doesn't do anything with them, worry about how to format them on the screen or anything else. It just – as the verb implies – gets. Stop-Service does just that: Stops a service. It doesn't care about where the services came from, and it doesn't even create any output by default. Export-CSV creates a CSV file, but has no idea where the data came from. If you force yourself to stick to the official PowerShell command name verbs, you'll be on the right track. (For that list, see http://msdn.microsoft.com/en-us/library/ms714428(v=vs.85).aspx) If you're writing a function that uses the verb "Get," which is an officially approved verb, then the cmdlet shouldn't do anything but get. It shouldn't put the information into the database, create an HTML file or anything else. It's just getting. Whatever it gets goes into the pipeline, and another cmdlet can then be used to output it, format it, filter it or do whatever might be needed at the time.

Along the same lines, a function should not use, within itself, cmdlets that aren't compatible with the function's own verb. For example, don't write a "Get" function that internally uses Format-Table to force the function's output into appearing as a table. Doing so prevents the cmdlet's output from being used for any other purpose in the future, and breaks the principal design goal of "just do one thing." In that case, the cmdlet is both getting and formatting, which is a poor practice.

Conclusion
We've added about as much functionality to the parameters of this function as we can. Now, it's time to start refining the function, making it more robust, and further customizing its output.

Error Handling

Error handling is covered in Learn Windows PowerShell in a Month of Lunches, but this chapter will go into a bit more detail. First, understand that there are two types of error handling available in PowerShell. The first is from version 1, and I don't especially like it because it's overly complicated and not as flexible as the approach introduced in version 2. So I'll mainly focus on that new approach, although I'll also show you the original approach, so you know what it is when you see it used elsewhere.

The purpose of error handling is to anticipate some kind of error condition and write your own set of instructions for what to do about it.

It's All About the Action

In PowerShell, cmdlets can encounter two types of errors: Terminating and non-terminating. A terminating error, also called an exception, is the only kind you can trap; non-terminating errors pass by without you being able to do anything about it. Most of the errors you might anticipate happening – access denied, file not found, computer not reachable and so forth – are non-terminating. For example, try this:

Seeing a Non-Terminating Error

```
01 Get-WmiObject -class Win32_BIOS -computerName
   localhost,notonline,localhost
```

There's an error message displayed for the nonexistent "notonline" computer, but the cmdlet keeps trucking along anyway. That happens due to the shell's built-in $ErrorActionPreference variable, which is by default set to "Continue". Whenever a cmdlet runs into a non-terminating error, it looks at the setting of $ErrorActionPreference to see what it should do. There are four possible settings:

- Inquire: Prompt the user to see what to do.
- Continue: Display an error and keep doing.
- SilentlyContinue: Don't display an error and keep going. (This is the setting I wish many small children possessed – "Be quiet, keep going.")
- Stop: Produce a terminating error and quit.

So the basic idea is that whenever you anticipate an error, you set the error action to "Stop". That way, any non-terminating errors become trappable exceptions.

Setting the Error Action

Unfortunately, dig up some scripts on the Internet (perhaps at http://poshcode.org, a popular community script repository) and you'll too often see this right at the top of the script:

Never Do This

```
01 $ErrorActionPreference = 'SilentlyContinue'
```

I hate that. What this is doing is telling the shell to suppress all errors produced by that entire script. My dentist tells me I have to stop looking at scripts like that, because I'm cracking my molars by grinding them so hard. I can't believe that anyone, ever, has produced a script so perfect that they can simply suppress all error messages for all time. People do this in the completely misguided belief that it's the right thing to do – and they're wrong, wrong, wrong. Don't ever do this.

A quick note: Putting that line of code in a script doesn't affect the default shell-wide $ErrorActionPreference. Variables, you'll recall, are scoped elements. Putting this line into a script creates a new $ErrorActionPreference within that script's scope, so it will only affect commands that run within that script. Once the script finishes, its scope is discarded, and the new $ErrorActionPreference is discarded with it, leaving the shell's original $ErrorActionPreference in place. But setting that variable is still the wrong thing to do.

It's easy to see how people can overlook the right way, though, because it's a bit buried. Take a look at the help for any cmdlet - say, Stop-Service. See the last thing in the syntax? It's "<CommonParameters>", a reference to a set of parameters that are present on every cmdlet because they're added by the shell itself. Read the "about_common_parameters" help topic and you'll see two common parameters that we've already used: -Verbose and -Debug. The common parameter for error handling is -ErrorAction, and it lets you specify an alternate error action for a single cmdlet, overriding $ErrorActionPreference for just that cmdlet. This is how you can suppress errors for a single command, and how you can convert non-terminating errors into full exceptions for trapping.

For example, consider (actually, try running) the following two commands:

Modifying the Error Action

```
01 Del c:\test.txt -ErrorAction SilentlyContinue
02 Get-WmiObject -class Win32_BIOS -computerName
   localhost,notonline,localhost -EA Stop
```

You'll notice in the second command that I used -EA, an alias for -ErrorAction. The first command runs without error, even if C:\test.txt doesn't exist. That's because I've suppressed errors for just that one command by setting its ErrorAction to SilentlyContinue. For the second command, I set the ErrorAction to Stop. That means it produces an exception and stops running; it never tries to contact localhost the second time. I didn't trap the error, so it just appeared on the screen. But I could trap that exception if I wanted.

Saving the Error

One more common parameter I will highlight is -ErrorVariable, which uses the alias -EV. Give it a variable name (not including the leading $) and it will store any error in that variable. That way, you have access to whatever error occurred.

Saving the Error

```
01 Del c:\test.txt -EA Stop -EV myError
02 Write $myError
```

There's also a built-in shell variable that contains all recent errors; you can access the first item in that variable's collection to get to the most recent error. That's useful when executing a method because methods don't have an -EV parameter. Examine the VARIABLE: drive in PowerShell and see if you can spot the built-in variable that holds errors.

Error Handling v1: The Trap Construct

This technique was mentioned at the outset of this chapter. It's one I don't like very much, although in v1 of PowerShell it's all we had to work with. It still works in v2 and looks something like this:

Listing 4-1: The Trap Construct

```
01 trap {
02   Write "An error occurred."
03   continue
04 }
05 $computers = @('localhost',
06                'notonline',
07                'localhost')
08 foreach ($computer in $computers) {
09   Get-WmiObject -class Win32_BIOS -computerName $computer -EA Stop
```

```
10 }
```

Take a look at that short script and see if you can predict what the output will be. Then run it and see if you're right.

Here's how this works:

- The Trap construct must be declared before any exceptions occur. PowerShell won't "scan ahead" in your script to look for a trap; when an exception occurs, PowerShell must have seen the trap, so that it knows where to jump to.

- The Trap constitutes its own scope. That means you have to be very careful about modifying any variables when you're inside the Trap construct.

- If the Trap ends in "break," then whatever exception occurred will be passed to the parent scope, and the current scope will terminate. In this case, it would mean the script stops running, and the exception would be passed to the shell.

- If the Trap ends to "continue," then execution will resume on the line following the one that caused the exception.

The trick with these is to make sure that any given command is only doing one thing at a time. That's why I put my computer names into an array, and then enumerated that array: This way, Get-WmiObject is only working with one computer name at a time. So if one computer name fails, the Continue keyword will be able to go back and resume the ForEach loop to get the next computer name.

It's possible to write multiple Trap constructs, each handling a specific type of exception. That way, different errors can be dealt with in different ways. For details on this, and examples, read the "about_trap" help topic in the shell.

Trap is closely tied to the scope hierarchy in the shell. For example, when an exception occurs, PowerShell looks to see if a Trap construct is defined within the current scope, be it a function, a script or something else. If there is a trap defined, then that Trap executes, and how it ends – using Break or Continue – determines if execution remains in that scope. However, if the current scope has no Trap, the exception will pass to the parent, and the current scope will be discarded. This can get awfully tricky. Consider this example:

Listing 4-2: Traps and Scope

```
01 trap {
02    Write "Trappped in script scope"
03    Continue
04 }
05 function Foo {
```

```
06   Write "In Foo"
07   Del C:\whatever.txt -EA Stop
08   Write "Still in Foo"
09 }
10 Write "Running the script"
11 Foo
12 Write "Ran the script"
```

Can you predict the output of that script? Try running it, and you'll find that the order of execution goes something like this:

0. Line 10 is the first executable command.

1. Line 11 runs next. This calls the function Foo.

2. Line 6 runs next.

3. Line 7 runs and produces an exception (assuming "whatever.txt" doesn't exist, which it shouldn't).

4. There's no Trap in the scope of function Foo, so execution passes up to the parent scope, which is the script. There is a Trap in the script's scope, so line 2 is the next that will execute.

5. Line 3 continues execution on the line after the one that caused the exception – but staying within the current scope. The current scope is the script; the script "sees" the problem as having come from line 11, so the next line is line 12. So line 12 executes.

6. The script finishes.

Line 8, in other words, never executed. This can get incredibly hard to keep track of, and it's one reason I don't much care for the Trap construct.

Try...Catch...Finally

This is the error handling that PowerShell team members wanted for v1, but didn't have time to get it working before they had to ship. They introduced it in v2, and with no reason to use v1 anymore, this is the type of error handling I think everyone should use.

This still relies on the -ErrorAction parameter being set to Stop but offers a more concise and flexible error handling construct. It looks something like this:

Try...Catch...Finally Pattern

```
01 Try {
02   # error-producing commands go here
03 } Catch {
04   # do something about the error here
05 } Finally {
06   # this executes whether an error or not
```

07 }

The Try block includes the command or commands that you believe might cause an error. You have to make sure to put "-EA Stop" on those commands so that any non-terminating errors become true, trappable exceptions.

What comes next depends on what you need to do.

In almost all cases, you'll use a Catch block, which is what PowerShell will execute if an exception occurs. Use -ErrorVariable with your command to capture the error, if needed. You can also specify multiple Catch blocks, with each one being set to "catch" a specific kind of exception. Read the "about_try_catch*" help topic for examples on how to do that.

You may want to include a Finally block, which will execute after Catch, and which will execute whether or not an error occurs. You don't see Finally used much, to be honest, but it's there if needed. You must have either Catch, Finally or both in conjunction with Try.

These constructs don't produce their own scope, so it's much easier to work with variables within them. I'll update Get-DJOSInfo to include error handling. I'm actually going to add quite a bit to the script: I'll start by adding an -errorLog parameter, which will accept a complete path and filename where I want failed computer names to be logged. In the function's setup routine, I'll make sure that error log is deleted, so that I'm not appending to a log from a previous attempt. Finally, I'll add error handling to my first Get-WmiObject call, logging the name of any computer that produces an error.

Notice that I'm setting a $continue variable, which will be $False if an error occurs. That lets me skip the subsequent WMI calls – after all, if the first one didn't work there's no reason to think the next two will.

Listing 4-3: Adding Error Handling to our Function

```
01 function Get-DJOSInfo {
02   [CmdletBinding()]
03   param (
04     [Parameter(Mandatory=$True,
05         ValueFromPipeline=$True,
06         ValueFromPipelineByPropertyName=$True,
07             HelpMessage='One or more computer names to query')]
08     [Alias('host')]
09     [ValidateNotNullorEmpty()]
10     [string[]]$computerName,
11
12     [Parameter(
13             HelpMessage='Write attempted computer names to a log')]
14     [switch]$nameLog,
15
16       [Parameter(
```

```
17              HelpMessage='Path and file to write failed computer
   names to')]
18      [string]$errorLog = 'c:\errors.txt'
19  )
20  BEGIN {
21    Write-Verbose 'Setting name log filename'
22    $i = 0
23    Do {
24      $i++
25      $logFile = "names-$i.txt"
26      Write-Verbose "Trying $logFile"
27    } While (Test-Path $logFile)
28    New-Variable -name nameLogFile -Value $logFile
29    Write-Verbose "Filename is $logFile"
30    Write-Verbose "Deleting $errorlog"
31    Del $errorlog –EA SilentlyContinue
32  }
33  PROCESS {
34    Write-Verbose "Starting PROCESS block"
35    if ($nameLog) {
36      Write-Debug 'Name logging on'
37    } else {
38      Write-Debug 'Name logging off'
39    }
40    foreach ($computer in $computerName) {
41      if ($nameLog) {
42        Write-Debug "Logging $computer to $nameLogFile"
43        $computer | Out-File $nameLogFile -append
44      }
45      Write-Debug "computer: $computer"
46      Write-Verbose "Querying WMI on $computer (step 1)"
47        $continue = $True
48        try {
49            $os = Get-WmiObject -computerName $computer -class
   Win32_OperatingSystem -EA Stop
50        } catch {
51            Write-Verbose "Query to $computer failed; logging to
   $errorlog"
52            $computer | Out-File -FilePath $errorLog -append
53            $continue = $false
54      }
55      if ($continue) {
56          Write-Verbose "Querying WMI on $computer (step 2)"
57          $bios = Get-WmiObject -computerName $computer -class
   Win32_BIOS
58          Write-Verbose "Querying WMI on $computer (step 3)"
59          $proc = Get-WmiObject -computerName $computer -class
   Win32_Processor | Select-Object -first 1
60          if ($os.osarchitecture -like '*64*') {
61            $osarch = 64
62                Write-Debug "OS Architecture 64 bit"
63          } else {
64                Write-Debug "OS Architecture 32 bit"
65            $osarch = 32
66          }
67          $data = @{
68            'ComputerName'=$computer;
```

```
69              'SPVersion'=$os.servicepackmajorversion;
70              'OSName'=$os.caption;
71              'OSArchitecture'=$osarch;
72              'OSBuild'=$os.buildnumber;
73              'ProcArchitecture'=$proc.addresswidth;
74              'BIOSSerial'=$bios.serialnumber
75          }
76              Write-Verbose 'Writing output to pipeline'
77          Write-Output (
78              New-Object -Type PSObject -Prop $data
79          )
80          }
81      }
82  }
83  END {}
84 }
85
```

Give that function a test run to see how it performs. As you start adding error handling to your own functions, be very careful to consider the logic of the entire script. For example, if my first Get-WmiObject command fails for some reason, then the entire remainder of the function is useless, right? I can't very well start creating output when more than a third of my desired data is missing. So that is why I have to trap any error from that first Get-WmiObject, and it's why any error means I'm basically going to skip the rest of the function.

Consider this alternative, which is something I see folks occasionally try to do. Can you figure out what would be wrong with this approach?

Listing 4-4: Improper Use of Error Handling

```
01 function Get-DJOSInfo {
02   [CmdletBinding()]
03   param (
04     [Parameter(Mandatory=$True,
05         ValueFromPipeline=$True,
06         ValueFromPipelineByPropertyName=$True,
07             HelpMessage='One or more computer names to query')]
08     [Alias('host')]
09     [ValidateNotNullorEmpty()]
10     [string[]]$computerName,
11
12     [Parameter(
13             HelpMessage='Write attempted computer names to a log')]
14     [switch]$nameLog,
15
16     [Parameter(
17             HelpMessage='Path and file to write failed computer
   names to')]
18     [string]$errorLog = 'c:\errors.txt'
19   )
20   BEGIN {
21     Write-Verbose 'Setting name log filename'
22     $i = 0
23     Do {
```

```
24    $i++
25    $logFile = "names-$i.txt"
26    Write-Verbose "Trying $logFile"
27    } While (Test-Path $logFile)
28    New-Variable -name nameLogFile -Value $logFile
29    Write-Verbose "Filename is $logFile"
30    Write-Verbose "Deleting $errorlog"
31    Del $errorlog -EA SilentlyContinue
32    }
33   PROCESS {
34    Write-Verbose "Starting PROCESS block"
35    if ($nameLog) {
36      Write-Debug 'Name logging on'
37    } else {
38      Write-Debug 'Name logging off'
39    }
40    foreach ($computer in $computerName) {
41      if ($nameLog) {
42        Write-Debug "Logging $computer to $nameLogFile"
43        $computer | Out-File $nameLogFile -append
44      }
45      Write-Debug "computer: $computer"
46      Write-Verbose "Querying WMI on $computer"
47        $continue = $True
48        try {
49            $os = Get-WmiObject -computerName $computer -class
Win32_OperatingSystem -EA Stop
50          $bios = Get-WmiObject -computerName $computer -class
Win32_BIOS
51          $proc = Get-WmiObject -computerName $computer -class
Win32_Processor | Select-Object -first 1
52        } catch {
53            Write-Verbose "Query to $computer failed; logging to
$errorlog"
54            $computer | Out-File -FilePath $errorLog -append
55            $continue = $false
56        }
57          if ($os.osarchitecture -like '*64*') {
58            $osarch = 64
59              Write-Debug "OS Architecture 64 bit"
60          } else {
61              Write-Debug "OS Architecture 32 bit"
62            $osarch = 32
63          }
64          $data = @{
65            'ComputerName'=$computer;
66            'SPVersion'=$os.servicepackmajorversion;
67            'OSName'=$os.caption;
68            'OSArchitecture'=$osarch;
69            'OSBuild'=$os.buildnumber;
70            'ProcArchitecture'=$proc.addresswidth;
71            'BIOSSerial'=$bios.serialnumber
72          }
73              Write-Verbose 'Writing output to pipeline'
74          Write-Output (
75            New-Object -Type PSObject -Prop $data
76          )
```

```
77                    }
78    }
79    END {}
80 }
81
```

At the very least, this is wasting time. Putting all three `Get-WmiObject` calls in the Try block is pointless. We only need to try one of them to realize that a computer isn't online, isn't reachable or some other problem. There's no sense in waiting for all three `Get-WmiObject` calls to time out. Further, we're not actually handling the error. True, we're logging the failed computer name – but we're not appropriately altering the function's behavior. Even if one of the `Get-WmiObject` calls fails, we're still trying to construct output as if all three calls had succeeded. That will doubtless result in other errors down the line, as the shell tries to access a variable like $os, $bios or $proc, which at that point doesn't contain anything – or contains leftover data from a prior computer. Logic is everything when it comes to computers, so you have to be very careful to think about the flow of execution.

Debugging

We're going to take a bit of a break from Get-DJOSInfo. Since it's a perfectly working function (smile), there's no need to debug it! And this chapter will be about those less-than-perfect functions and scripts that you will inevitably write.

Two Types of Bugs

I broadly classify bugs into two categories: typos and logic errors.

Typos are just that: Human error. Fat fingers. Operation malfunction. Keyboard failure. Whatever you call it, it's fixable.

One way to prevent these things is to use a decent script editor – and the PowerShell ISE doesn't actually qualify as "decent" in this respect. It does offer color-coding, which can help you prevent many typos once you get used to the coloring. If you're typing, and the coloring isn't right, then you've got a typo.

On the other hand, a decent editor will often do more, including live syntax checking that gives you a red underline not unlike Word's live spell-check. Editors in this category include PrimalScript (www.sapien.com), PowerShell Plus (www.idera.com), PowerGUI (www.powergui.org), and so on.

There are certainly others. I list some of the major ones at www.ShellHub.com. Most offer a free trial to see which one you like best. You may spend some money, but the tools they give you – code completion, syntax checking and so forth – will save you time in debugging typos.

When typos inevitably creep in, you can – and should – read the error message. I know, it's the most obvious-sounding thing in the world. But the fact is that most of us don't read error messages. We see all that red text, flash back to high school English class and those marked-up essays and blank out. I've seen admins immediately type "Cls" just so no one will see the horrible error they've committed. Don't! Read the error! PowerShell often tells you the line number it's upset with, and that's where you start looking for your typo. I'll offer more tips in this chapter.

The other broad category of error is the logic bug, and this one is a lot more insidious. With these little devils, you don't get error messages, or you get errors that make no sense given what you're trying to do.

Normally, your script runs – just not the way you want. These errors, in my experience, come from one thing and one thing only: bad assumptions. Perhaps you thought a property contained "True" when in fact it contains "0" (which the shell interprets as False). Maybe you've got a variable that you thought contained a computer name – but for some reason it just contains a comma. Most of debugging involves tracing down these bad assumptions and correcting them, and that's what this chapter is about.

The key here is having an expectation for what your script should do, line by line, in the first place. All I can do in this chapter is show you how to validate your expectations and see where they differ from reality. If you don't have an expectation for what each line of your script will do, you can't debug a script. Period.

Solving Typos

Because typos are preventable (just don't mistype anything, ever), I won't spend a great deal of time on this topic. However, I do want to offer some quick tips to help you interpret some of the trickier error messages that typos can cause. For example, try running this:

Listing 5-1: Tricky Typo Errors

```
01 function Foo {
02 if ((Read-Host "Enter a number") -eq 5 {
03 Write-Host 'You entered 5'
04 } else {
05 Write-Host 'You didn't enter 5'
06 }
```

Run this and the error messages won't always point you to the place where the problem actually exists. For example, the first error will probably point to the end of line 2, indicating that PowerShell encountered a { character when it was expecting a) character – because I missed the) that closed the If construct's expression.

The next error, assuming you fix the first one, will probably be on line 6. That's the end of the script, and PowerShell will have been expecting a } to close the function. Take a careful look at that error message and get used to it, because you'll probably see it a lot if you produce scripts with formatting as atrocious as Listing 5-1. Let's look at that function again, with the first error corrected and with nicer formatting.

Listing 5-2: Tricky Typo Errors, Redux

```
01 function Foo {
02   if ((Read-Host "Enter a number") -eq 5) {
03     Write-Host 'You entered 5'
04   } else {
05     Write-Host 'You didn't enter 5'
```

```
06   }
```

See? It's a lot more visually obvious that something – the function's closing } – is missing. This is exactly why people indent constructs in this fashion – to make it easier to confirm they've all been closed properly. Again, a good editor can help. For example, PowerShell Plus automatically creates the closing } when you type the opening {, so it's a lot harder to mess up.

Don't look at the error messages PowerShell produces and give up. Read them, and try to understand them. Try to think like the shell. When it says "I expected to see }, and I didn't," it's telling you something.

Dealing with Logic Errors: Trace Code

Now to the bulk of this chapter. Again, the real goal of debugging is to identify the places in which your expectations for your script differ from the reality of your script. Those differences are likely bugs. Once you identify where your expectations are wrong (because it's always your fault, not the script's), you can implement fixes.

So the way we implement debugging is through a couple of techniques designed to let us see "inside" the script, compare it to our expectations and see if we were right or not.

The first of these techniques is called "adding trace code." Many a VBScript programmer can tell you tales of adding "Wscript.Echo" calls to their script for this exact purpose. I often see PowerShell newcomers using Write-Host to produce trace output – although, as I've mentioned elsewhere, using Write-Host is an indication that your soul is in jeopardy. It's just the wrong thing to do.

Instead, PowerShell gives us Write-Debug – something you've already seen in an earlier chapter of this book. Earlier, I used it inside an advanced function, meaning I could run the function with -Debug to turn on that output. In other circumstances, PowerShell won't automatically implement a -Debug parameter for you, so you'll have to manually turn on Write-Debug's output. To do so, just pop this into the first line of your script, function or whatever:

Turning on Debug Output

```
01 $DebugPreference = 'Continue'
```

That's it. With that at the top of a script or function (in a function, it must appear after any Param() block), Write-Debug will operate. Comment out, or delete, that line, and debug output will be suppressed. So you don't have to go through your script removing all of the Write-Debug statements when you're done debugging! Just leave them in there, on the very good odds that you'll have to modify that script in the future, will probably break it again and will need to debug again. In fact, as I also mentioned earlier, I tend to write my Write-Debug statements as I write a script or function in the first place, assuming that I'll get something wrong and will need to debug.

I've said that logic errors tend to result from you believing that a property, or a variable, contained something other than it really contained. Write-Debug is therefore a way to find out what those really contain. There are a couple of tricks to using it, though.

First off, let's take the straightforward need to output the contents of a variable, assuming those contents are a single, basic value like a string or number.

Write-Debug: Simple Values in a Variable

```
01 Write-Debug "`$computer = $computer"
```

Notice the back tick escape character before the first dollar sign? That preserves the dollar sign as a literal character for that instance, so that the result will be something like "$computer = SERVER2".

This same trick doesn't work if you need to access the contents of a property, because dotted-notation syntax doesn't work with the variable-replacement trick. The easiest fix is to just put the property into a variable.

Write-Debug: Property Contents

```
01 $temp = $object.property
02 Write-Debug "Property is $temp"
```

If you need to look at the contents of a collection, meaning you need to see multiple objects... well, that's more difficult. Write-Debug can't handle an entire object, let alone a collection of them. Here's an example of what you could do as a workaround.

Write-Debug: Collection of Objects

```
01 $services = Get-Service
02 foreach ($service in $service) {
03   $sname = $service.name
04   $sstatus = $service.status
05   Write-Debug "$sname is status $sstatus"
06 }
```

Not quite beautiful, but functional. The basic idea is: Whatever you want to debug, you put into a variable by itself and then add that variable to the Write-Debug text.

I mentioned earlier in this book that I don't have a hard-and-fast line between Write-Verbose and Write-Debug, except that I generally like my verbose output to mean something to someone else, while my debug output only has to have meaning to me – and even then, only when I'm debugging. I'm not even always consistent about those rules, and sometimes my fingers type "Write-Verbose", when they should have typed "Write-Debug".

Dealing with Logic Errors: Breakpoints

One problem with debug (or verbose) output is that it can create a lot of clutter. What if you have a 300-line function, and you just know that its problem is somewhere near line 250? Do you really want to wade through the output from the first 249 lines before you start dealing with the problem?

Perhaps not – and that's why breakpoints are so helpful. Now, let's be clear about something: I'm only going cover breakpoints as they're implemented in PowerShell itself. There's support for those in both the console and in the PowerShell ISE. Third-party editors often have similar functionality, but they often implement it on their own, and their breakpoints may work somewhat differently. Although I won't be covering those, I think they can be quite valuable – third parties often add convenience features and capabilities that beat the shell's built-in breakpoint functionality.

A breakpoint is simply a trigger that makes the shell pause but not stop whatever it was doing. The shell drops into a special "suspended" mode, which some folks call "debug mode," in which you can run commands, check the contents of variables, and so forth. The advantage of this mode is that you remain inside whatever scope the shell was executing, so variables and other scoped elements will appear exactly as the shell currently sees them.

PowerShell lets you set breakpoints in a number of ways:

- When a given command is executed
- When a variable is read, changed or either of those
- When execution reaches a certain line (and optionally, a certain column) of a script

Those first two can be set globally for the shell, or they can be set to only affect a particular script. When setting a breakpoint on a script, the shell identifies the script by its exact path and filename. That means if you change the path and/or filename, the breakpoint will stop working.

Within the ISE, you can use a shortcut key to set a line breakpoint. The ISE will helpfully color that line in dark red, and if you run the script from within the ISE it will pause appropriately. Within the console window, the shell provides several commands for managing breakpoints. (These can also be run within the ISE, although there's no graphical equivalent or shortcut key for them.) They are:

Commands for Managing Breakpoints

```
01 Get-Command -noun PSBreakpoint
```

Let's walk through a quick example. Don't bother typing these scripts in – I'll keep them short, so you can run through them "in your head," rather than actually executing them in the shell. The first is just a sample script that I'll add some breakpoints to in a moment.

Listing 5-3: C:\Debug.ps1

```
01 function Debug-Me {
02   param (
03     $computerName
04   )
05   $disk = Get-WmiObject -class Win32_LogicalDisk -computerName
      $computerName
06   $os = Get-WmiObject -class Win32_OperatingSystem -computerName
      $computerName
07   $props = @{
08     'ComputerName'=$computerName;
09     'FreeSpace'=$disk.freespace;
10     'Size'=$disk.size;
11     'OSBuild'=$os.buildnumber
12   }
13   $obj = New-Object -type PSObject -prop $props
14   Write $obj
15 }
16 Debug-Me -comp localhost
```

Run that, and it will likely spew all kinds of errors. But DON'T run it – instead, walk through it and develop an expectation. What do you think each line of this script will actually accomplish?

The first error will probably be around line 7, so let's set a breakpoint there.

Setting a Breakpoint

```
01 Set-PSBreakpoint -script c:\Debug.ps1 -line 7
```

Running the script again, I would see the shell "pause" before executing line 7. I want to take that opportunity to quickly check the contents of the variables up to that point. Remember, errors generally occur because a property or variable contained something other than what you expected. I expect $disk to contain a disk drive object, and $os to contain an operating system object. In suspend mode, here's what I see when I check them:

Using Suspend Mode

```
01 PS C:\> ./debug
02 Entering debug mode. Use h or ? for help.
03
04 Hit Line breakpoint on 'C:\Debug.ps1:7'
05
06 debug.ps1:7       $props = @{
07 [DBG]: PS C:\>>> $computername
08 localhost
09 [DBG]: PS C:\>>> $disk
10
11
12 DeviceID      : A:
13 DriveType     : 2
14 ProviderName  :
15 FreeSpace     :
16 Size          :
17 VolumeName    :
18
19 DeviceID      : C:
20 DriveType     : 3
21 ProviderName  :
22 FreeSpace     : 32243634176
23 Size          : 42842714112
24 VolumeName    :
25
26 DeviceID      : D:
27 DriveType     : 5
28 ProviderName  :
29 FreeSpace     :
30 Size          :
31 VolumeName    :
32
33
34
35 [DBG]: PS C:\>>>
```

Not quite what I expected. This is a subtle error that a lot of newcomers make, though. You see, my $disk variable does not contain a disk drive object – it contains several of them. That makes sense; line 5 is certainly querying all of them, without filtering any out. Most computers will contain a couple (or more) drives, and so I'm getting them all.

The problem is that line 7's hash table attempts to access the FreeSpace and Size properties of multiple objects. You can't do that. Imagine that you're standing in the middle of a car lot, and I ask you, "what color is the car?" Your first response would be, "Which car?" That's exactly how PowerShell feels about line 7 (or, more accurately, lines 9 and 10). "Which disk did you want the size and free space for? I've got several here to choose from." I have a couple of ways I could fix this – but for right now, I'll let the script finish crashing so that I can then fix it.

Exiting Suspend Mode

```
01 [DBG]: PS C:\>>> exit
```

I'm just going to make a minor modification to line 5 of the script.

Modifying the Script

```
01   $disk = Get-WmiObject -class Win32_LogicalDisk -computerName
     $computerName -filter "DeviceID='C:'"
```

Now, I'm expecting this to only return one disk – the one with the device ID (or drive letter) "C:". I'll re-run the script again, and again I'll hit that breakpoint.

Using Suspend Mode, Redux

```
01 PS C:\> ./debug
02 Hit Line breakpoint on 'C:\Debug.ps1:7'
03
04 debug.ps1:7        $props = @{
05 [DBG]: PS C:\>>> $computername
06 localhost
07 [DBG]: PS C:\>>> $disk
08
09
10 DeviceID      : C:
11 DriveType     : 3
12 ProviderName  :
13 FreeSpace     : 32243642368
14 Size          : 42842714112
15 VolumeName    :
```

This time, I got what I expected – a single disk. I'll run Exit again to let the script continue, and this time it should finish without error. Now that I've fixed it, I can remove the breakpoint:

Removing Breakpoints

```
03 Get-PSBreakpoint | Remove-PSBreakpoint
```

That's the basic process for debugging: Get an expectation, find a way to verify the expectation and make corrections wherever you find your expectation was incorrect.

The Real Trick to Debugging

Although Write-Debug, Write-Verbose, and breakpoints are all valuable debugging tools, they're useless without knowledge. You cannot debug a script unless you know, or at least think you know, what it's supposed to do. I find that to be the biggest challenge with PowerShell. Most administrators have been insulated from the technology by layers of GUIs, so they really don't know how the technology works, which makes it difficult to debug. You develop your expectations not based on what's happening under the hood, but based on what the GUI usually does for you. Until you become more knowledgeable about the underlying technology, PowerShell – and debugging – will always seem more difficult than it should. The upside is if you become really good in PowerShell, it's because you're also getting smarter about the technology – and that will make you a better administrator all-around.

Custom Formatting

Run a couple of native PowerShell cmdlets, such as Get-Service or Get-Process. Like what you see?

Most PowerShell command's default output is controlled by a set of ".format.ps1xml" files. For built-in PowerShell cmdlets, these files are in PowerShell's installation folder, under C:\Windows\System32\WindowsPowerShell\v1.0.

For add-in modules, the XML files are generally in the module's own folders. These XML files contain view definitions, which lay out the default lists, tables, and other views that you see when you run a command and don't specify any formatting instructions of your own. Use a Format cmdlet, or Select-Object, and you'll generally be overriding the defaults with your own instructions.

Without an XML-defined view, PowerShell's formatting rules are pretty simple: Give it an object with four or fewer properties and it displays a table that tries to fill the width of the screen, adding blank space between columns to spread everything out. Five or more properties get you a list. But that's just the default.

The Anatomy of a View

First of all, before I even tell you what to do next, let me issue a strong word of caution.

Do not modify the .format.ps1xml files provided to you by Microsoft or other vendors. And by "do not modify" I mean "don't even add an extra space or carriage return." Microsoft digitally signs their files, and the slightest modification will break that signature – significantly impacting the way the shell operates for you. It's fine to look at these files; just don't press "Save" at any time.

Okay, with that out of the way, go ahead and use Notepad to open one.

Examining a View File

```
01 cd $pshome
02 notepad dotnettypes.format.ps1xml
```

Now use Notepad's Find function to look for "System.Diagnostics.Process". The first hit will probably be a "System.Diagnostics.ProcessModule", which is not what you want; hit

Find again to get to a the plain Process one. There are a few things I'd like you to look out for:

- Each view is "selected by" a particular object type name. That is, when PowerShell has objects in the pipeline that it needs to format, it does so by getting the object's TypeName and looking for a corresponding view. When you run Get-Process, the result is a bunch of System.Diagnostics.Process objects in the pipeline, which is how this view gets called into play.

- For a table view, you can have a section that specifies the column headers, widths, and alignment. You also get a section that specifies column contents, which can be simple properties, or even complex calculations.

- List views are similar, but less complex since you don't have to format the columns. Scroll in the XML file a bit until you find a list view – pay attention to the tag names and you'll spot the list type of view.

The sad news is that these XML files aren't well-documented. The good news is that copy and paste, plus a little experimentation, can do wonders. We'll use Microsoft's XML file as a template for creating our own. Be careful, though: While most of PowerShell isn't case-sensitive, these XML files definitely are. Upper and lowercase must be strictly observed.

Adding a Type Name to Output Objects
Before we start making an XML file, we have to look at the output of Get-DJOSInfo. Unfortunately, right now the output is just a PSObject. That's the generic object type we created for our output. Unfortunately, we can't assign a custom view to that type because it's used everywhere in the shell. In order to have a custom view for just our output, we've got to give our output a custom type name. We'll then use that type name to trigger a view. Adding a type name is easy.

Listing 6-1: Adding a Custom Type Name

```
01 function Get-DJOSInfo {
02   [CmdletBinding()]
03   param (
04     [Parameter(Mandatory=$True,
05         ValueFromPipeline=$True,
06         ValueFromPipelineByPropertyName=$True,
07             HelpMessage='One or more computer names to query')]
08     [Alias('host')]
09     [ValidateNotNullorEmpty()]
10   [string[]]$computerName,
11
12     [Parameter(
```

```
13                  HelpMessage='Write attempted computer names to a log')]
14      [switch]$nameLog,
15
16      [Parameter(
17                  HelpMessage='Path and file to write failed computer
   names to')]
18      [string]$errorLog = 'c:\errors.txt'
19    )
20  BEGIN {
21    Write-Verbose 'Setting name log filename'
22    $i = 0
23    Do {
24      $i++
25      $logFile = "names-$i.txt"
26      Write-Verbose "Trying $logFile"
27    } While (Test-Path $logFile)
28    New-Variable -name nameLogFile -Value $logFile
29    Write-Verbose "Filename is $logFile"
30    Write-Verbose "Deleting $errorlog"
31    Del $errorlog -EA SilentlyContinue
32  }
33  PROCESS {
34    Write-Verbose "Starting PROCESS block"
35    if ($nameLog) {
36      Write-Debug 'Name logging on'
37    } else {
38      Write-Debug 'Name logging off'
39    }
40    foreach ($computer in $computerName) {
41      if ($nameLog) {
42        Write-Debug "Logging $computer to $nameLogFile"
43        $computer | Out-File $nameLogFile -append
44      }
45      Write-Debug "computer: $computer"
46      Write-Verbose "Querying WMI on $computer (step 1)"
47        $continue = $True
48        try {
49                $os = Get-WmiObject -computerName $computer -class
   Win32_OperatingSystem -EA Stop
50        } catch {
51                Write-Verbose "Query to $computer failed; logging to
   $errorlog"
52                $computer | Out-File -FilePath $errorLog -append
53                $continue = $false
54        }
55        if ($continue) {
56            Write-Verbose "Querying WMI on $computer (step 2)"
57            $bios = Get-WmiObject -computerName $computer -class
   Win32_BIOS
58            Write-Verbose "Querying WMI on $computer (step 3)"
59            $proc = Get-WmiObject -computerName $computer -class
   Win32_Processor | Select-Object -first 1
60            if ($os.osarchitecture -like '*64*') {
61              $osarch = 64
62                    Write-Debug "OS Architecture 64 bit"
63            } else {
64                    Write-Debug "OS Architecture 32 bit"
```

```
65                $osarch = 32
66              }
67              $data = @{
68                'ComputerName'=$computer;
69                'SPVersion'=$os.servicepackmajorversion;
70                'OSName'=$os.caption;
71                'OSArchitecture'=$osarch;
72                'OSBuild'=$os.buildnumber;
73                'ProcArchitecture'=$proc.addresswidth;
74                'BIOSSerial'=$bios.serialnumber
75              }
76                  Write-Verbose 'Writing output to pipeline'
77              $obj = New-Object -Type PSObject -Prop $data
78
    $obj.PSObject.TypeNames.Insert(0,'Don.InventoryObject')
79                  Write-Output $obj
80              }
81       }
82     }
83   END {}
84 }
```

Immediately after creating my output object, and just before writing it to the pipeline, I've given it a custom type name. This can literally be anything you want, although you should give it a "custom namespace" type of name, as I did, so that there's less chance of it overlapping with some other type name that already exists somewhere in the .NET Framework. To test, pipe the output of the function to Get-Member. (Remember that you have to dot-source the script into the shell in order to make the Get-DJOSInfo function available to run. I'm assuming this script is in C:\Scripts\Tools.ps1 but it may be something like Listing6-1.ps1 on your computer.)

Testing the Type Name

```
01 Del FUNCTION:\Get-DJOSInfo –EA SilentlyContinue
02 . C:\Scripts\Tools.ps1
03 Get-DJOSInfo -comp localhost | Get-Member
```

If the TypeName shown by Get-Member is the correct custom type name, then you're good to go.

Making a View

Next, we'll make a custom view in a brand-new text file. Again, be careful of upper and lower case letters! XML is case-sensitive!

Listing 6-2: Custom View File

```
01 <?xml version="1.0" encoding="utf-8" ?>
02
03 <Configuration>
04     <ViewDefinitions>
```

```
05 <View>
06              <Name>Inventory</Name>
07              <ViewSelectedBy>
08                  <TypeName>Don.InventoryObject</TypeName>
09              </ViewSelectedBy>
10              <TableControl>
11                  <TableHeaders>
12                      <TableColumnHeader>
13                          <Label>ComputerName</Label>
14                          <Width>20</Width>
15                          <Alignment>left</Alignment>
16                      </TableColumnHeader>
17                      <TableColumnHeader>
18                          <Label>OS</Label>
19                          <Width>2</Width>
20                          <Alignment>right</Alignment>
21                      </TableColumnHeader>
22                      <TableColumnHeader>
23                          <Label>Proc</Label>
24                          <Width>4</Width>
25                          <Alignment>right</Alignment>
26                      </TableColumnHeader>
27                  </TableHeaders>
28                  <TableRowEntries>
29                      <TableRowEntry>
30                          <TableColumnItems>
31                              <TableColumnItem>
32
   <PropertyName>ComputerName</PropertyName>
33                              </TableColumnItem>
34                              <TableColumnItem>
35
   <PropertyName>OSArchitecture</PropertyName>
36                              </TableColumnItem>
37                              <TableColumnItem>
38
   <PropertyName>ProcArchitecture</PropertyName>
39                              </TableColumnItem>
40                          </TableColumnItems>
41                      </TableRowEntry>
42                  </TableRowEntries>
43              </TableControl>
44          </View>          </ViewDefinitions>
45 </Configuration>
```

Notice that I gave my view a name? I'll explain why in the next section.

I'll save this in the same folder as the script, naming it
DonJonesTypes.format.ps1xml. Be very careful if you're using Notepad to
edit this file because Notepad likes to add a ".txt" filename extension to
everything. Double-check your filename in PowerShell to make sure it's
correct. You can also edit these XML files in the PowerShell ISE, which
won't add extraneous stuff to the filename.

Loading the View

With the view file saved to disk, we need to load it into the shell's memory. The command to do so, Update-FormatData, offers two options: We can have our view loaded before what's already in memory, or we can load it after what's already in memory. These options are referred to as prepending and appending, respectively.

PowerShell actually permits you to define multiple views for a single type. When the shell needs to display an object, it uses the first view that is "selected by" the object's type. So, if you want your view to be the shell's default, your view must be the first one it finds in memory – hence the "prepend" option.

Alternately, you can place your view later in memory, using the "append" option. That means your view won't be used by default if another view "selected by" the same object TypeName is already in memory. However, your view could still be selected manually, by using its name. Process objects are actually a good example of this: DotNetTypes.format.ps1xml actually contains more than one view for System.Diagnostics.Process objects. Only the first gets used by default, but you could manually select an alternate if you know its view name:

Manually Selecting an Alternate View

```
01 PS C:\> get-process | format-table -view priority
02
03
04     PriorityClass: Normal
05
06 ProcessName           Id  HandleCount   WorkingSet
07 -----------           --  -----------   ----------
08 conhost             1936           53      5779456
09 csrss                328          346      1105920
10 csrss                376          263      2588672
11 explorer            1868          732     19562496
12 ...
```

The downside of alternate views is that PowerShell doesn't currently offer any way to discover which ones are available – you pretty much have to be told by someone else, or find it on your own by browsing through those XML files. You do browse through the XML files, right? No, I didn't think so – which is why alternate views aren't well-known.

Anyway, our new custom view should be the only one of its kind for our custom object type, so it won't matter if we prepend or append. Let's just load it in memory and try it out. (Don't forget – you need to make sure that the version of Get-DJOSInfo that's loaded into your shell is producing objects with the custom type name.)

Loading the Custom View

```
01 Update-FormatData -append C:\Scripts\DonJonesTypes.format.ps1xml
02 Get-DJOSInfo -comp localhost
```

Pretty cool, right?

If you try this and get a bunch of error messages, don't panic. Take a moment and read the errors – they'll point you to the line that's causing the problem. In all likelihood, you incorrectly capitalized something, forgot to close an XML tag or some similar kind of typo-related error. Fix the problem and try again.

One caveat: "Try again" means "close PowerShell, open a new shell window, and try again." There's an annoying behavior in PowerShell that makes the shell think the view is loaded, even though the load failed. Because it thinks the file is loaded, you can't try to load it again, and there's no way to unload it. Experimenting with view files thus means a lot of opening and closing of shell windows. I like to put view files in a short directory path – like C:\ – while I'm experimenting, just so I have less to type as I continuously reload files.

Problems at this Point

Cool as it may be, we're starting to run into a lot of hassle. Let me outline the problems with the point I've brought you to:

- Every time we change Get-DJOSInfo, we have to delete the old copy of the function from the FUNCTION: drive, and then re-dot-source the script.

- We also have to dot-source the script every time we open a new shell session.

- Now, we also have to remember to run Update-FormatData every time we change the XML file, or every time we open a new shell session.

There are too many things to remember to do. We need to do away with dot-sourcing and move to a more sophisticated means of loading our script.

Script and Manifest Modules

This business of manually loading multiple related files – our script and its format view file – is painful. Having to delete functions from the FUNCTION: drive is also painful. Fortunately, PowerShell offers a better way: Modules.

Introducing Modules

There are basically three kinds of modules. Before I cover them, however, let's talk about how these things are stored.

When PowerShell v2 is installed on a computer, it creates a computer-wide environment variable called PSModulePath. This environment variable tells PowerShell where modules are kept. It's perfectly fine to keep a module outside the path or paths in the environment variable; to load one of those "rogue" modules you simply provide a complete path and filename to it. However, by keeping modules in the official locations, you can load them by simply specifying a module name. You can modify the PSModulePath environment variable if you want to add another "official" location, such as a shared location that you and your colleagues all use.

By default, PSModulePath contains a single path for your own modules: ..\[My]Documents\WindowsPowerShell\Modules. In other words, within your Documents folder (which on older versions of Windows is "My Documents"), you create a folder named WindowsPowerShell (no spaces). Under that, you create a folder named Modules.

Now for the tricky bit, or at least the bit people tend to get wrong a lot. You have to come up with a name for your module, ideally one that doesn't include spaces (simply because you'd have to use quotation marks if it included spaces). Let's say we're going to name our new module MyTools. That means we first have to create a folder named MyTools:

Module Folder Hierarchy

```
01 /Users/<username>/[My ]Documents
02    WindowsPowerShell
03       Modules
04          MyTools
05             Tools.psm1
06             DonJonesTypes.format.ps1xml
```

Into that folder, I've copied both the script containing Get-DJOSInfo (which was tools.ps1, now renamed tools.psm1) and my new custom view file (DonJonesTypes.format.ps1xml). The ".psm1" filename extension represents a script module, and enables the correct loading and unloading behavior within the shell.

When you load a module, perhaps by running "Import-Module MyTools," PowerShell looks for three files in a specific order:

0. First, it looks for MyTools.psd1. This is a manifest file, and it enables the shell to load modules that include multiple files.

1. Second, it looks for MyTools.dll. This is a binary module, produced in Visual Studio by a VB or C# developer.

2. Third, it looks for MyTools.psm1. This is a script module, produced in PowerShell itself. It's really just a plain old script with a different filename extension.

You can see that my current contents of MyTools doesn't contain any of these files. I could just rename Tools.ps1 to MyTools.psm1, and PowerShell would find it and load it as a script module. But I also want it to load my custom view, so instead I'll create a module manifest named MyTools.psd1.

The crucial thing here is that the module's name must appear both in the folder, and in the filename of the file you want loaded. Since my module is named MyTools, I need the folder to be MyTools and the manifest to be MyTools.psd1.

Creating a Module Manifest

PowerShell's New-ModuleManifest cmdlet will create the manifest for me. It requires a good bit of information about my new module, and enables me to specify all of the files I want the module to load.

Creating the Module Manifest

```
01 PS C:\> New-ModuleManifest
02
03 cmdlet New-ModuleManifest at command pipeline position 1
04 Supply values for the following parameters:
05 Path:
   c:\users\administrator\documents\windowspowershell\modules\mytools\My
   Tools.psd1
06 NestedModules[0]:
07 Author: Don Jones
08 CompanyName: Concentrated Technology
09 Copyright: 2011 by Don Jones
10 ModuleToProcess: MyTools.psm1
11 Description: A test module manifest
12 TypesToProcess[0]:
```

```
13 FormatsToProcess[0]: DonJonesTypes.format.ps1xml
14 FormatsToProcess[1]:
15 RequiredAssemblies[0]:
16 FileList[0]:
17 PS C:\>
```

Note that I ran the New-ModuleManifest cmdlet without any parameters, and
let the shell prompt for me what it wanted. On items where I didn't have
anything to specify, I just hit Enter. Go ahead and look at the resulting
.psd1 file in Notepad, just to see what it contains. It's okay to modify that
file manually if you want to change something – you don't need to use the
cmdlet each time.

Now it's time to test the module. I'm going to completely close my
PowerShell window so that I can get a fresh start, and then try my new
module.

Loading a Module

```
01 Import-Module MyTools
02 Get-DJOSInfo -comp localhost
```

If I did everything correctly, I'll get my custom-formatted results.

Creating a Module-Level Setting Variable

You're probably used to some of PowerShell's built-in variables, like
$ErrorActionPreference, that act as shell-wide configuration settings.
Modules can do something similar, by creating their own global variables.
By placing a variable into the global scope, you make it easy for users to
find and change that variable. By using that variable within your module's
functions, you can effectively create the same kind of configuration
settings that the shell itself uses.

I'll use this technique to create a global-level variable that has a default
path and filename for my functions' error log files.

Listing 7-1: Creating a Configuration Setting for a Module

```
01 $DJDefaultErrorLog = 'c:\errors.txt'
02 function Get-DJOSInfo {
03   [CmdletBinding()]
04   param (
05     [Parameter(Mandatory=$True,
06         ValueFromPipeline=$True,
07         ValueFromPipelineByPropertyName=$True,
08             HelpMessage='One or more computer names to query')]
09       [Alias('host')]
10       [ValidateNotNullorEmpty()]
11     [string[]]$computerName,
12
13     [Parameter(
14             HelpMessage='Write attempted computer names to a log')]
```

```
15      [switch]$nameLog,
16
17      [Parameter(
18              HelpMessage='Path and file to write failed computer
  names to')]
19      [string]$errorLog = $DJDefaultErrorLog
20   )
21  BEGIN {
22    Write-Verbose 'Setting name log filename'
23    $i = 0
24    Do {
25      $i++
26      $logFile = "names-$i.txt"
27      Write-Verbose "Trying $logFile"
28    } While (Test-Path $logFile)
29    New-Variable -name nameLogFile -Value $logFile
30    Write-Verbose "Filename is $logFile"
31    Write-Verbose "Deleting $errorlog"
32    Del $errorlog -EA SilentlyContinue
33  }
34  PROCESS {
35    Write-Verbose "Starting PROCESS block"
36    if ($nameLog) {
37      Write-Debug 'Name logging on'
38    } else {
39      Write-Debug 'Name logging off'
40    }
41    foreach ($computer in $computerName) {
42      if ($nameLog) {
43        Write-Debug "Logging $computer to $nameLogFile"
44        $computer | Out-File $nameLogFile -append
45      }
46      Write-Debug "computer: $computer"
47      Write-Verbose "Querying WMI on $computer (step 1)"
48      $continue = $True
49      try {
50            $os = Get-WmiObject -computerName $computer -class
  Win32_OperatingSystem -EA Stop
51        } catch {
52            Write-Verbose "Query to $computer failed; logging to
  $errorlog"
53            $computer | Out-File -FilePath $errorLog -append
54            $continue = $false
55        }
56      if ($continue) {
57          Write-Verbose "Querying WMI on $computer (step 2)"
58          $bios = Get-WmiObject -computerName $computer -class
  Win32_BIOS
59          Write-Verbose "Querying WMI on $computer (step 3)"
60          $proc = Get-WmiObject -computerName $computer -class
  Win32_Processor | Select-Object -first 1
61          if ($os.osarchitecture -like '*64*') {
62             $osarch = 64
63                  Write-Debug "OS Architecture 64 bit"
64          } else {
65                  Write-Debug "OS Architecture 32 bit"
66             $osarch = 32
```

```
67                }
68                $data = @{
69                    'ComputerName'=$computer;
70                    'SPVersion'=$os.servicepackmajorversion;
71                    'OSName'=$os.caption;
72                    'OSArchitecture'=$osarch;
73                    'OSBuild'=$os.buildnumber;
74                    'ProcArchitecture'=$proc.addresswidth;
75                    'BIOSSerial'=$bios.serialnumber
76                }
77                    Write-Verbose 'Writing output to pipeline'
78                $obj = New-Object -Type PSObject -Prop $data
79
   $obj.PSObject.TypeNames.Insert(0,'Don.InventoryObject')
80                    Write-Output $obj
81                }
82      }
83    }
84    END {}
85 }
```

By the way, from this point in the book forward, I'll assume that you're working with the MyTools module. That means subsequent listings will provide a complete replacement for the Tools.psm1 file. If you're working with downloaded script files (provided at http://MoreLunches.com), you'd just copy and rename Listing7-1.ps1 to \Documents\WindowsPowerShell\Modules\MyTools\Tools.psm1, overwriting the older version of Tools.psm1. You'll have to do that with every new listing from here on out. The good news is that you're done with dot sourcing!

Notice that I've selected a variable name that has a DJ prefix, so it's less likely to conflict with variables created by other modules, or by the shell itself. I've got a problem, though: Right now, this variable exists only within the scope of this script file, so it won't be seen by shell users. I could make it a global-level variable, but if I did that, it would stick around even if my module was unloaded using Remove-Module, and I don't want to leave orphaned variables behind.

The solution is to export the variable. Doing so will turn it into a global variable when my module is loaded, and enable the shell to keep track of the variable so that it can be removed if the module is unloaded. The problem is that once you start exporting things from a module, you have to export everything that you want made visible to users of the module. Anything you fail to export will be hidden. So if I'm going to export this variable, I also need to export my Get-DJOSInfo function.

Listing 7-2: Exporting a Variable and a Function

```
01 $DJDefaultErrorLog = 'c:\errors.txt'
02
03 function Get-DJOSInfo {
04    [CmdletBinding()]
```

```
05  param (
06     [Parameter(Mandatory=$True,
07         ValueFromPipeline=$True,
08         ValueFromPipelineByPropertyName=$True,
09             HelpMessage='One or more computer names to query')]
10     [Alias('host')]
11     [ValidateNotNullorEmpty()]
12     [string[]]$computerName,
13
14     [Parameter(
15             HelpMessage='Write attempted computer names to a log')]
16     [switch]$nameLog,
17
18     [Parameter(
19             HelpMessage='Path and file to write failed computer
    names to')]
20     [string]$errorLog = $DJDefaultErrorLog
21  )
22  BEGIN {
23    Write-Verbose 'Setting name log filename'
24    $i = 0
25    Do {
26      $i++
27      $logFile = "names-$i.txt"
28      Write-Verbose "Trying $logFile"
29    } While (Test-Path $logFile)
30    New-Variable -name nameLogFile -Value $logFile
31    Write-Verbose "Filename is $logFile"
32    Write-Verbose "Deleting $errorlog"
33    Del $errorlog -EA SilentlyContinue
34  }
35  PROCESS {
36    Write-Verbose "Starting PROCESS block"
37    if ($nameLog) {
38      Write-Debug 'Name logging on'
39    } else {
40      Write-Debug 'Name logging off'
41    }
42    foreach ($computer in $computerName) {
43      if ($nameLog) {
44        Write-Debug "Logging $computer to $nameLogFile"
45        $computer | Out-File $nameLogFile -append
46      }
47      Write-Debug "computer: $computer"
48      Write-Verbose "Querying WMI on $computer (step 1)"
49        $continue = $True
50        try {
51            $os = Get-WmiObject -computerName $computer -class
    Win32_OperatingSystem -EA Stop
52        } catch {
53            Write-Verbose "Query to $computer failed; logging to
    $errorlog"
54            $computer | Out-File -FilePath $errorLog -append
55            $continue = $false
56        }
57        if ($continue) {
58            Write-Verbose "Querying WMI on $computer (step 2)"
```

```
59              $bios = Get-WmiObject -computerName $computer -class
   Win32_BIOS
60              Write-Verbose "Querying WMI on $computer (step 3)"
61              $proc = Get-WmiObject -computerName $computer -class
   Win32_Processor | Select-Object -first 1
62              if ($os.osarchitecture -like '*64*') {
63                  $osarch = 64
64                      Write-Debug "OS Architecture 64 bit"
65              } else {
66                      Write-Debug "OS Architecture 32 bit"
67                  $osarch = 32
68              }
69              $data = @{
70                  'ComputerName'=$computer;
71                  'SPVersion'=$os.servicepackmajorversion;
72                  'OSName'=$os.caption;
73                  'OSArchitecture'=$osarch;
74                  'OSBuild'=$os.buildnumber;
75                  'ProcArchitecture'=$proc.addresswidth;
76                  'BIOSSerial'=$bios.serialnumber
77              }
78                  Write-Verbose 'Writing output to pipeline'
79              $obj = New-Object -Type PSObject -Prop $data
80
   $obj.PSObject.TypeNames.Insert(0,'Don.InventoryObject')
81                  Write-Output $obj
82              }
83      }
84  }
85  END {}
86 }
87
88 Export-ModuleMember -Function Get-DJOSInfo
89 Export-ModuleMember -Variable DJDefaultErrorLog
```

Take a close look at the bottom of the script, and you'll see where I export both the variable and the function. It's technically possible to do both exports in a single call to Export-ModuleMember, but I like doing one thing at a time just for neater formatting. Note that it's also possible to export these items in the manifest; I tend to prefer putting the Export-ModuleMember calls into the script module file because it's a more visible reminder of what I'm doing. It's easy to forget what's in the manifest, and cumbersome to have to update it every time I add something to the file.

Also notice that I've modified Get-DJOSInfo slightly. In my parameter declaration, I've set the -errorLog parameter to have a default of whatever is in $DJDefaultErrorLog. That way, if someone runs Get-DJOSInfo without specifying -errorLog, the parameter will just use whatever is in that exported variable.

I've deliberately followed PowerShell naming conventions for that exported variable. In addition to using a "DJ" prefix to help avoid naming conflicts, I've named this variable to correspond with the parameter that it provides the default for: -errorLog.

At this point, close your copy of PowerShell, import the MyTools module, and try running the function – both with and without an -errorLog parameter. See if it works as desired.

Testing the Module

```
01 # (after opening a fresh shell window)
02 Import-Module MyTools
03 Get-DJOSInfo -comp localhost,x -verbose
04 $DJErrorLogPreference = 'c:\err2.txt'
05 Get-DJOSInfo -comp localhost,x -verbose
06 Get-DJOSInfo -comp localhost,x -errorLog c:\e.txt -verbose
```

If everything looks good, you're ready to move on. Make sure that the verbose output of the above commands reflects the appropriate error log filename. Also, make sure that the indicated log file was actually created, and that each one contains "x", the name of the computer that doesn't exist.

Writing Help

With your MyTools module loaded into the shell, try asking for help on the Get-DJOSInfo function.

Asking for Help on a Function

```
01 Help Get-DJOSInfo
02
03 # alternately...
04 Get-DJOSInfo -?
05
06 # also try this...
07 Help Get-DJOSInfo -full
```

The results aren't awful. PowerShell parses our parameter declarations to construct a reasonable syntax page. But it's hardly the full, robust help we're used to seeing from a PowerShell cmdlet.

It pains me, but I frequently see admins laboriously constructing their own "-?" parameter for their functions. They'll spend hours writing Write-Host commands that reproduce the nicely formatted look of PowerShell's own help. Sadly, they're wasting time. Anytime you're using Write-Host, in fact, you're probably wasting your time. "If you use Write-Host," I continually tell students, "you're probably going to Hell." My Twitter followers (@concentrateddon) even have a #powershellProverbs hash tag for those kinds of sayings.

Let's add some great-looking help to that function... but let's make PowerShell do the hard work, shall we?

Comment-Based Help

The first and easiest way to add help is to use comment-based help. Read the "about_comment_based_help" topic for more details on this, although the following example will show you the basics:

Listing 8-1: Adding Comment-Based Help

```
01 $DJDefaultErrorLog = 'c:\errors.txt'
02
03 function Get-DJOSInfo {
04 <#
05 .SYNOPSIS
06 Retrieves key inventory information from one or more computers.
07 .DESCRIPTION
08 This command uses WMI to retrieve key information about one or
```

```
09 more computers. Computer names or IP addresses can be piped in,
10 or specified on the -computerName parameter.
11 .PARAMETER computerName
12 The computer name (or names) to query.
13 .PARAMETER nameLog
14 Using this switch forces all attempted computer names to be
15 logged to a uniquely-named text file.
16 .PARAMETER errorLog
17 Specify the path and filename of a text file to which failed
18 computer names should be logged. Defaults to the contents of
19 the $DJDefaultErrorLog variable.
20 .EXAMPLE
21 Get-DJOSInfo -computerName SERVER-R2 -nameLog -verbose
22 .EXAMPLE
23 Get-Content names.txt | Get-DJOSInfo
24 #>
25   [CmdletBinding()]
26   param (
27     [Parameter(Mandatory=$True,
28         ValueFromPipeline=$True,
29         ValueFromPipelineByPropertyName=$True,
30             HelpMessage='One or more computer names to query')]
31     [Alias('host')]
32     [ValidateNotNullorEmpty()]
33    [string[]]$computerName,
34
35     [Parameter(
36             HelpMessage='Write attempted computer names to a log')]
37     [switch]$nameLog,
38
39      [Parameter(
40             HelpMessage='Path and file to write failed computer
   names to')]
41      [string]$errorLog = $DJDefaultErrorLog
42   )
43   BEGIN {
44    Write-Verbose 'Setting name log filename'
45    $i = 0
46    Do {
47      $i++
48      $logFile = "names-$i.txt"
49      Write-Verbose "Trying $logFile"
50    } While (Test-Path $logFile)
51    New-Variable -name nameLogFile -Value $logFile
52    Write-Verbose "Filename is $logFile"
53    Write-Verbose "Deleting $errorlog"
54    Del $errorlog -EA SilentlyContinue
55   }
56   PROCESS {
57     Write-Verbose "Starting PROCESS block"
58     if ($nameLog) {
59       Write-Debug 'Name logging on'
60     } else {
61       Write-Debug 'Name logging off'
62     }
63     foreach ($computer in $computerName) {
64       if ($nameLog) {
65         Write-Debug "Logging $computer to $nameLogFile"
```

```
66          $computer | Out-File $nameLogFile -append
67        }
68      Write-Debug "computer: $computer"
69      Write-Verbose "Querying WMI on $computer (step 1)"
70        $continue = $True
71        try {
72              $os = Get-WmiObject -computerName $computer -class
    Win32_OperatingSystem -EA Stop
73        } catch {
74              Write-Verbose "Query to $computer failed; logging to
    $errorlog"
75              $computer | Out-File -FilePath $errorLog -append
76              $continue = $false
77        }
78        if ($continue) {
79            Write-Verbose "Querying WMI on $computer (step 2)"
80            $bios = Get-WmiObject -computerName $computer -class
    Win32_BIOS
81            Write-Verbose "Querying WMI on $computer (step 3)"
82            $proc = Get-WmiObject -computerName $computer -class
    Win32_Processor | Select-Object -first 1
83            if ($os.osarchitecture -like '*64*') {
84              $osarch = 64
85                    Write-Debug "OS Architecture 64 bit"
86            } else {
87                    Write-Debug "OS Architecture 32 bit"
88              $osarch = 32
89            }
90            $data = @{
91              'ComputerName'=$computer;
92              'SPVersion'=$os.servicepackmajorversion;
93              'OSName'=$os.caption;
94              'OSArchitecture'=$osarch;
95              'OSBuild'=$os.buildnumber;
96              'ProcArchitecture'=$proc.addresswidth;
97              'BIOSSerial'=$bios.serialnumber
98            }
99                Write-Verbose 'Writing output to pipeline'
100                   $obj = New-Object -Type PSObject -Prop $data
101
    $obj.PSObject.TypeNames.Insert(0,'Don.InventoryObject')
102                   Write-Output $obj
103              }
104        }
105      }
106    END {}
107  }
108
109  Export-ModuleMember -Function Get-DJOSInfo
110  Export-ModuleMember -Variable DJDefaultErrorLog
```

That comment-based help takes the form of a block <# comment #>, which must appear either immediately prior to, or immediately after, the function name declaration. I tend to put the help inside the function, although some people prefer to put it just before. Using special dotted keywords (which don't have to be uppercase, although I think they stand out nicely that way), you define the sections of the "help file." Try it out (again assuming that you've renamed and copied Listing8-1.ps1 to \Documents\WindowsPowerShell\Modules\MyTools\tools.psm1):

Testing Comment-Based Help

```
01 Remove-Module MyTools
02 Import-Module MyTools
03 MyTools -?
04 Help MyTools -full
```

Pretty cool, right?

Comment-based help is easy, and lets you include everything from parameter descriptions to examples. Its only real downside is that it only supports a single language. If you want to provide help in more than one language (perhaps you have colleagues in Germany and Japan), you'll have to use PowerShell's full, XML-based help file format.

XML-Based Help

PowerShell's native help system uses an XML format called MAML, which is a bit of a bear to work with. The upside is that it does support multiple languages, and will default to the language that Windows is configured to use. This help is contained in an external file, too, which helps keep your functions a bit shorter and more readable by moving the help out of those sometimes-lengthy comments.

There are a couple of ways to make working with MAML a bit easier. One is to use Microsoft InfoPath, along with an InfoPath template. You'll find details, and the template, at http://blogs.technet.com/b/jamesone/archive/2009/07/24/powershell-on-line-help-a-change-you-should-make-for-v2-3-and-how-to-author-maml-help-files-for-powershell.aspx.

Note that you can't use the file output by InfoPath; you do have to make a minor adjustment to it in order for PowerShell to use the file properly. The blog post I've linked explains what you'll need to do.

Another option is to download a cmdlet help editor, http://blogs.msdn.com/b/powershell/archive/2011/02/24/cmdlet-help-editor-v2-0-with-module-support.aspx.

This tool essentially lets you copy and paste the bits of your help (synopsis, description and so forth), and produces a ready-to-use MAML file.

Each XML file contains the help for a single language. You then have to create the proper folder structure. Assume you've created U.S. English help, and German help, all for the MyTools module we're building:

Folder Structure for Help

```
01 \Users\<username>\[My ]Documents
02    \WindowsPowerShell
03      \Modules
04        \MyTools
05          tools.psm1
06          DonJonesTypes.format.ps1xml
07          MyTools.psd1
08          \<en-US>
09            MyTools-help.xml
10            about_MyTools.txt
11          \<de-DE>
12            MyTools-help.xml
13            about_MyTools.txt
```

The English help goes under the <en-US> folder, while the German help goes under <de-DE>. Those two folder names reflect the internal "culture codes" that Windows uses to identify a language (such as "en" or "de") and its regional variants (such as "US" or, for British English, "UK"). One thing you should know is that many international PowerShell users actually use a US English version of Windows, so their default help language is en-US. I'm told by some folks at Microsoft that, although the company provides PowerShell help in more than a dozen languages, the en-US ones are used most often. Before translating help files into languages other than US English, check with the folks who will be using that help to confirm which language(s) they want.

Notice that I've also specified an "about" topic for the entire module, which is just a plain text file. That file has to have the filename "about_<moduleName>.txt" where <moduleName> is the exact name of your module – "MyTools" in our running example. I've also provided an XML file, in each language, which contains help for the individual functions. Those XML files are created using the PowerShell Help Editor tool (or InfoPath, if you prefer). You can add as many languages as you want, provided each is included in a folder with the proper culture name.

The XML-based help definitely requires a bit more effort. It's worth it if you have (or want to write) extensive help that makes comment-based help unwieldy, or if you want to provide help in multiple languages for a given module.

Using Databases

In this chapter, we'll start working with SQL Server. Everything you learn here will actually work almost identically with any other database for which you have .NET Framework-compatible database drivers. I'll point out specific differences as we come to them.

For this chapter, I'll assume that your computer has SQL Server Express installed, along with the Express Management Tools. That stuff is all free, and can be downloaded from Microsoft's Web site. I'll also expect that you've installed it using the default installation options, too, meaning that SQL Server is accessible at localhost\SQLEXPRESS.

Examples in this chapter may help you pick up the basics of the SQL language, but I'm assuming that you already understand them. There are several great books and training videos that can help you learn SQL language basics. In fact, my video series for CBT Nuggets (http://cbtnuggets.com) covers the SQL language as it applies to almost any SQL-compatible platform, including Microsoft SQL Server.

This chapter will not focus on database administration, creating new databases, programming databases or any of that. We'll be focused solely on accessing the data in a database. Further, I'll be using a very simplified technique that provides the highest cross-compatibility with different database products, and which requires the least amount of coding. If you're familiar with other .NET Framework database access techniques – like data adaptors, data tables, and so on – you're free to use those, but I won't be covering them here. If you already know how to use those, then you should be fine on your own because they work the same way in PowerShell as they do in VB or C#.

Simplifying Database Access

As I stated in the introduction to this book, I'm drawing an arbitrary line at using the .NET Framework directly from within PowerShell.

In order to access databases, we have to use the Framework directly; in order to stick with this book's stated goals, I'll give you some functions that wrap around the underlying Framework classes and simplify them a bit. If you have the desire, these very straightforward functions can be torn apart and the pieces used directly within your scripts. Otherwise, you can simply use them as-is. I'm not even going to make these functions especially beautiful because I don't intend for anyone to use them except for me. I'm not going to go through all the work of declaring fancy parameters, or adding help or anything else. I refer to these as "utility functions," and when I add them to my module I'll hide them so that only the functions within my module – and nothing outside my module – can see them.

I'll use a couple of different database access techniques within these functions, and I'll walk through each of them at the end of this chapter to explain how they work. As written, these functions will work solely with Microsoft SQL Server, although I'll point out the very minor changes needed to make them work with nearly any other kind of database.

Setting Up Your Environment

As I mentioned, I'm assuming that you have a copy of SQL Server Express to work with. You can get one, for free, from http://download.microsoft.com; just punch in "SQL Express" into the search box. Microsoft releases new versions of SQL Server Express at the same time as other editions of the product, so make sure you're grabbing the latest version that will run on your computer. For my examples, I'm using SQL Server 2008 R2 SP1 Express Edition, but that may not be the latest available by the time you read this. Be sure to download the correct build (32-bit is "x86" and 64-bit is "x64") also.

There's often an option to download a package that includes tools. Those will be listed as "WT", "with tools" or something similar. If possible, get that version. If you can't find it, Microsoft sometimes offers SQL Server Express in one download, and "Management Studio Express" in a separate download that you can search for. Again, make sure to get the right 32-bit or 64-bit build for your computer.

Accept the defaults when installing the product. SQL Server is designed to have many copies, or *instances,* running on a single computer; by default, SQL Server Express generally installs a *named instance* called SqlExpress, as shown in the screen capture below. You'll have a chance to change this during installation – but don't. Seriously, just take the defaults for everything, so that you'll be able to follow the exact examples I'll give you.

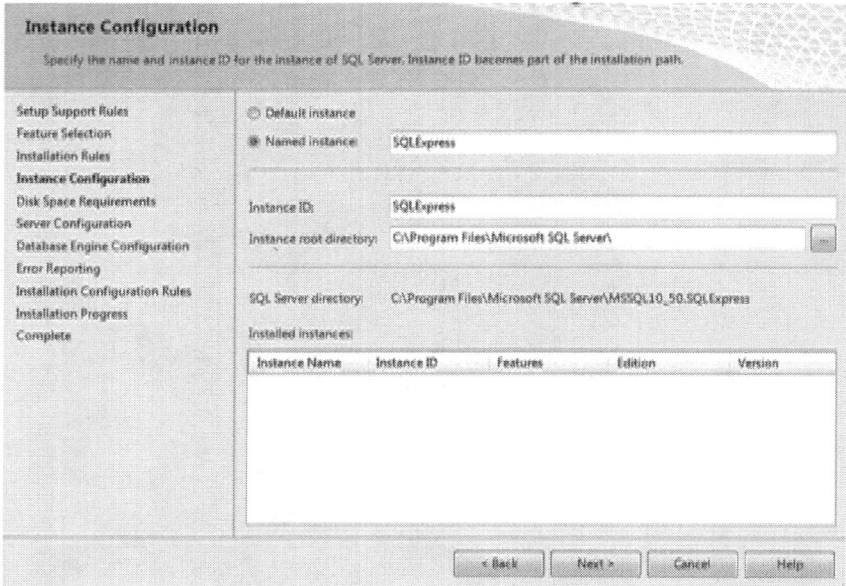

After installing, go to PowerShell and verify the instance name by looking at the list of installed services:

Verifying the SQL Server Express Instance Name

```
01 PS C:\Users\Administrator> get-service -name *sql*
02
03 Status     Name                DisplayName
04 ------     ----                -----------
05 Stopped    MSSQL$SQLEXPRESS     SQL Server (SQLEXPRESS)
06 Stopped    MSSQLServerADHe...   SQL Active Directory Helper Service
07 Stopped    SQLAgent$SQLEXP...   SQL Server Agent (SQLEXPRESS)
08 Stopped    SQLBrowser           SQL Server Browser
09 Running    SQLWriter            SQL Server VSS Writer
```

Those services with (SQLEXPRESS) in the DisplayName are what I'm after. Notice that the key service here, MSSQL$SQLEXPRESS, is stopped: That will need to be started in order for SQL Server to actually work. That's the only service that needs to be running for basic functionality.

```
01 PS C:\Users\Administrator> start-service 'mssql$sqlexpress'
```

Now, we need to make a database to play with. On your Start Menu, locate SQL Server Management Studio and open it. If you installed SQL Server using the defaults, you should be able to connect like this:

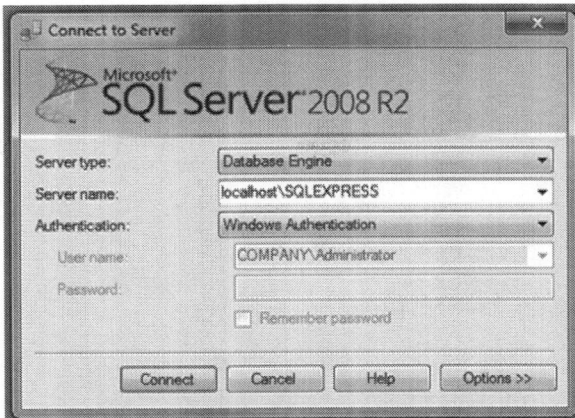

To keep this easy, immediately click the New Query button in the toolbar. I'll give you a SQL query that will create a new database and set up a new table within it.

Listing 9-1: Creating a Database

```
01  CREATE DATABASE [Inventory] ON  PRIMARY
02 ( NAME = N'Inventory', FILENAME = N'c:\Program Files\Microsoft SQL
    Server\MSSQL10_50.SQLEXPRESS\MSSQL\DATA\Inventory.mdf' , SIZE =
    2048KB , FILEGROWTH = 1024KB )
03  LOG ON
04 ( NAME = N'Inventory_log', FILENAME = N'c:\Program Files\Microsoft
    SQL Server\MSSQL10_50.SQLEXPRESS\MSSQL\DATA\Inventory_log.ldf' , SIZE
    = 1024KB , FILEGROWTH = 10%)
05 GO
06 USE [Inventory]
07 GO
08 SET ANSI_NULLS ON
09 GO
10 SET QUOTED_IDENTIFIER ON
11 GO
12 CREATE TABLE [dbo].[Computers](
13      [computer] [nvarchar](50) NULL,
14      [osversion] [nvarchar](100) NULL,
15      [biosserial] [nvarchar](100) NULL,
16      [osarchitecture] [nvarchar](5) NULL,
17      [procarchitecture] [nvarchar](5) NULL
18 ) ON [PRIMARY]
19
20 GO
```

To run this, click the "! Execute" button in the toolbar. Make sure it runs without error.

Now we'll put a couple of rows of data into the database. Close the query window you were working in, and then open a new one by clicking that New Query button again.

Listing 9-2: Adding data to the database

```
01 Use [Inventory]
02 Go
03 INSERT INTO Computers (computer) VALUES ('localhost')
04 INSERT INTO Computers (computer) VALUES ('localhost')
05 INSERT INTO Computers (computer) VALUES ('not-online')
```

Once again, "! Execute" this query and make sure it runs without error.

The Database Functions

I'm going to give you two generic functions that can be used to query data from any database, or make changes to any database. For testing purposes, start by saving this script as C:\db.ps1.

Listing 9-3: C:\Db.ps1

```
01 function Get-DatabaseData {
02     [CmdletBinding()]
03     param (
04             [string]$connectionString,
05             [string]$query,
06             [switch]$isSQLServer
07     )
08     if ($isSQLServer) {
09             Write-Verbose 'in SQL Server mode'
10             $connection = New-Object -TypeName
   System.Data.SqlClient.SqlConnection
11     } else {
12             Write-Verbose 'in OleDB mode'
13             $connection = New-Object -TypeName
   System.Data.OleDb.OleDbConnection
14     }
15     $connection.ConnectionString = $connectionString
16     $command = $connection.CreateCommand()
17     $command.CommandText = $query
18     if ($isSQLServer) {
19             $adapter = New-Object -TypeName
   System.Data.SqlClient.SqlDataAdapter $command
20     } else {
21             $adapter = New-Object -TypeName
   System.Data.OleDb.OleDbDataAdapter $command
22     }
23     $dataset = New-Object -TypeName System.Data.DataSet
24     $adapter.Fill($dataset)
25     $dataset.Tables[0]
26 }
27 function Invoke-DatabaseQuery {
28     [CmdletBinding()]
29     param (
30             [string]$connectionString,
31             [string]$query,
32             [switch]$isSQLServer
33     )
```

```
34      if ($isSQLServer) {
35              Write-Verbose 'in SQL Server mode'
36              $connection = New-Object -TypeName
   System.Data.SqlClient.SqlConnection
37      } else {
38              Write-Verbose 'in OleDB mode'
39              $connection = New-Object -TypeName
   System.Data.OleDb.OleDbConnection
40      }
41      $connection.ConnectionString = $connectionString
42      $command = $connection.CreateCommand()
43      $command.CommandText = $query
44      $connection.Open()
45      $command.ExecuteNonQuery()
46      $connection.close()
47 }
```

Dot source this into the shell, and then test it to make sure you're able to run both functions without error:

Testing the Database Functions

```
01 . c:\db.ps1
02 Get-DatabaseData -verbose -connectionString
   'Server=localhost\SQLEXPRESS;Database=Inventory;Trusted_Connection=Tr
   ue;' -isSQLServer -query "SELECT * FROM Computers"
03 Invoke-DatabaseQuery -verbose -connectionString
   'Server=localhost\SQLEXPRESS;Database=Inventory;Trusted_Connection=Tr
   ue;' -isSQLServer -query "INSERT INTO Computers (computer)
   VALUES('win7')"
04 Get-DatabaseData -verbose -connectionString
   'Server=localhost\SQLEXPRESS;Database=Inventory;Trusted_Connection=Tr
   ue;' -isSQLServer -query "SELECT * FROM Computers"
```

Note that you shouldn't expect these to work if you didn't install SQL Server Express using the defaults. If you did use the defaults, however, and you've followed along in this chapter up to this point, then you should have seen some nice, non-error output.

With the testing out of the way, close your PowerShell console. Let's make these two functions into their own module. Simply re-save C:\Db.ps1 in your Documents folder as WindowsPowerShell\Modules\Database\Database.psm1.

Then, open WindowsPowerShell\Modules\MyTools\MyTools.psd1. We'll make a minor change to the module manifest. Find the line that starts with "NestedModules," which should be around line 66. Modify it to read as follows:

```
01 NestedModules = @('Database')
```

Save the .PSD1 file. Open a new PowerShell console, and try to import the MyTools module:

```
01 Import-Module MyTools
```

That should run without error. However, trying to run `Help Get-DatabaseData` should produce an error. That's because we have the MyTools module internally loading the Database module, but we don't have it exposing (or *exporting*) the two functions from the Database module. That's exactly what I want: I didn't dress up the two database functions as I normally do. They don't have help, their parameters don't have any attributes, and so forth – they're not intended for direct human consumption. As it sits, anything *inside* MyTools.psm1 will be able to use the two database functions, but that's all. They're *private*, in other words. You could still load the database functions for your own interactive use, simply by running `Import-Module Database`, if you want. Right now, I don't want to. Instead, I want to add some more functions to MyTools.psm1.

About the Database Functions

First, a little background on the two database functions. Get-DatabaseData is used when you want to query information from a database; Invoke-DatabaseQuery is used when you want to make changes, such as adding data, removing data or changing data. Each supports three parameters:

-ConnectionString
This tells PowerShell how to find the database server, what database to connect to, and how to authenticate. The example I provided in the test above will connect to the Inventory database of the localhost\SQLEXPRESS SQL Server instance. You can find more connection string examples at http://ConnectionStrings.com.

-isSQLServer
Include this switch when your connection string points to a Microsoft SQL Server. Omit this string for all other database server types, and PowerShell will use OleDB instead. You'll need to make sure your connection string is OleDB compatible, and that you've installed the necessary OleDB drivers to access your database. That can be MySQL, Access, Oracle or whatever you like.

-Query
This is the actual SQL language query that you want to run. To learn more about the SQL language, access my training video on the subject, which can be found at http://www.cbtnuggets.com/it-training-videos/series/cbtn_sql_lang.

Invoke-DatabaseQuery doesn't return any output; it just runs your query. Get-DatabaseData will retrieve data and place it into the pipeline. Within the pipeline, you'll get objects with properties that correspond to the columns of the database. So, in the example shown earlier, I got a "computer" property, a "biosserial" property, and so forth, because those are the columns from the Computers table of the Inventory database.

That's all the detail we'll cover on how the two database functions operate internally. As I said at the outset, the "line in the sand" for this book is the .NET Framework. These functions internally utilize the .NET Framework, and so for this book they're out of scope. The functions do, however, provide a nice wrapper around .NET, so that you can access databases without having to mess around with the raw .NET Framework stuff.

Using the Database Functions

Let's modify MyTools.psm1 to put those database functions to work. Below is a complete replacement for MyTools.psm1. Copy this script and replace your existing \WindowsPowerShell\Modules\MyTools\MyTools.psm1 file. Then, open a new PowerShell console and run Import-Module MyTools.

I'll point out that I haven't included comment-based help for the new functions in the module. That's mainly just to save space here – you should always include help when you add a new function to a module.

Just get this file in place, and then I'll explain the key bits.

Listing 9-4: New Functions for the MyTools Module

```
01  $DJDefaultErrorLog = 'c:\errors.txt'
02
03  function Get-DJOSInfo {
04      [CmdletBinding()]
05      param (
06          [Parameter(Mandatory=$True,
07              ValueFromPipeline=$True,
08              ValueFromPipelineByPropertyName=$True,
09                  HelpMessage='One or more computer names to query')]
10          [Alias('host')]
11          [ValidateNotNullorEmpty()]
12          [string[]]$computerName,
13
14          [Parameter(
15                  HelpMessage='Write attempted computer names to a log')]
16          [switch]$nameLog,
17
18          [Parameter(
19                  HelpMessage='Path and file to write failed computer
    names to')]
20          [string]$errorLog = $DJDefaultErrorLog
21      )
22  BEGIN {
23    Write-Verbose 'Setting name log filename'
24    $i = 0
25    Do {
26        $i++
27        $logFile = "names-$i.txt"
28        Write-Verbose "Trying $logFile"
29    } While (Test-Path $logFile)
```

```
30    New-Variable -name nameLogFile -Value $logFile
31    Write-Verbose "Filename is $logFile"
32    Write-Verbose "Deleting $errorlog"
33    Del $errorlog -EA SilentlyContinue
34    }
35    PROCESS {
36      Write-Verbose "Starting PROCESS block"
37      if ($nameLog) {
38          Write-Debug 'Name logging on'
39        } else {
40          Write-Debug 'Name logging off'
41        }
42      foreach ($computer in $computerName) {
43          if ($nameLog) {
44            Write-Debug "Logging $computer to $nameLogFile"
45            $computer | Out-File $nameLogFile -append
46          }
47          Write-Debug "computer: $computer"
48          Write-Verbose "Querying WMI on $computer (step 1)"
49          $continue = $True
50          try {
51                $os = Get-WmiObject -computerName $computer -class
      Win32_OperatingSystem -EA Stop
52          } catch {
53                Write-Verbose "Query to $computer failed; logging to
      $errorlog"
54                $computer | Out-File -FilePath $errorLog -append
55                $continue = $false
56          }
57          if ($continue) {
58              Write-Verbose "Querying WMI on $computer (step 2)"
59              $bios = Get-WmiObject -computerName $computer -class
      Win32_BIOS
60              Write-Verbose "Querying WMI on $computer (step 3)"
61              $proc = Get-WmiObject -computerName $computer -class
      Win32_Processor | Select-Object -first 1
62              if ($os.osarchitecture -like '*64*') {
63                $osarch = 64
64                    Write-Debug "OS Architecture 64 bit"
65              } else {
66                    Write-Debug "OS Architecture 32 bit"
67                $osarch = 32
68              }
69              $data = @{
70                'ComputerName'=$computer;
71                'SPVersion'=$os.servicepackmajorversion;
72                'OSName'=$os.caption;
73                'OSArchitecture'=$osarch;
74                'OSBuild'=$os.buildnumber;
75                'ProcArchitecture'=$proc.addresswidth;
76                'BIOSSerial'=$bios.serialnumber
77              }
78                  Write-Verbose 'Writing output to pipeline'
79              $obj = New-Object -Type PSObject -Prop $data
80
      $obj.PSObject.TypeNames.Insert(0,'Don.InventoryObject')
81                  Write-Output $obj
```

```
82                  }
83          }
84        }
85      END {}
86    }
87
88    function Get-DJComputersFromSQL {
89        [CmdletBinding()]
90        param (
91                  [Parameter(Mandatory=$true,
92                                      HelpMessage='SQL Server instance
    name')]
93                  [string]$SQLServer,
94
95                  [Parameter(Mandatory=$true,
96                                      HelpMessage='SQL Server database
    name')]
97                  [string]$Database,
98
99                  [Parameter(Mandatory=$true,
100                                     HelpMessage='SQL Server table
    name')]
101                 [string]$Table,
102
103                 [Parameter(Mandatory=$true,
104                                     HelpMessage='Column containing
    computer names')]
105                 [string]$Column
106       )
107
108       $connectionString =
    "Server=$SQLServer;Database=$Database;Trusted_Connection=True;"
109       Write-Verbose "Connection String: $connectionString"
110       $query = "SELECT $column FROM $table"
111       Write-Verbose "Query: $query"
112
113       Get-DatabaseData -connectionString $connectionString -
    isSQLServer -query $query |
114       Select-Object -Property
    @{name='computername';expression={$_.$column}}
115   }
116
117   function Set-DJComputersInSQL {
118       [CmdletBinding()]
119       param (
120                 [Parameter(Mandatory=$true,
121                                     HelpMessage='SQL Server instance
    name')]
122                 [string]$SQLServer,
123
124                 [Parameter(Mandatory=$true,
125                                     HelpMessage='SQL Server database
    name')]
126                 [string]$Database,
127
128                 [Parameter(Mandatory=$true,
129                                     HelpMessage='SQL Server table
    name')]
130                 [string]$Table,
```

```
131
132                [Parameter(Mandatory=$true,
133
     ValueFromPipelineByPropertyName=$true)]
134                [string]$osarchitecture,
135
136                [Parameter(Mandatory=$true,
137
     ValueFromPipelineByPropertyName=$true)]
138                [string]$procarchitecture,
139
140                    [Parameter(Mandatory=$true,
141
     ValueFromPipelineByPropertyName=$true)]
142                [string]$biosserial,
143
144                [Parameter(Mandatory=$true,
145
     ValueFromPipelineByPropertyName=$true)]
146                [string]$computername
147       )
148       PROCESS {
149                $connectionString =
     "Server=$SQLServer;Database=$Database;Trusted_Connection=True;"
150                Write-Verbose "Connection String: $connectionString"
151                $query = "UPDATE $table SET osarchitecture =
     '$osarchitecture', procarchitecture='$procarchitecture',
     biosserial='$biosserial' WHERE computer = '$computername'"
152                Write-Verbose "Query: $query"
153
154                Invoke-DatabaseQuery -connectionString
     $connectionString -isSQLServer -query $query |
155                Out-Null
156       }
157 }
158
159 Export-ModuleMember -Function Get-DJComputersFromSQL
160 Export-ModuleMember -Function Set-DJComputersInSQL
161 Export-ModuleMember -Function Get-DJOSInfo
162 Export-ModuleMember -Variable DJDefaultErrorLog
```

Okay, first take a look at lines 168 and 169. That's where I'm making the two new functions visible. Easy stuff.

Line 97 begins the first of the two new functions, whose job is to retrieve computer names from my inventory database. It's going to put them into the pipeline with a "computerName" property, regardless of what the database column name actually is. That way, the property name will line up with what my Get-DJOSInfo function is expecting.

Note that this is an advanced function, although it has no PROCESS block. I don't ever intend for this to accept pipeline input, and I haven't set up any parameter to accept pipeline input, so the PROCESS block isn't needed. Also notice how I'm having the function accept simple pieces of data, and then using those – with double quotation marks – to construct the actual connection string and query. I should acknowledge that constructing a SQL query by concatenating strings like this is potentially dangerous because it opens the way for a kind of attack known as *SQL injection.* However, these functions are only to be used by a trusted administrator, so I've chosen not to worry about it.

I'm using Write-Verbose to output the final connection string and query; this will let me check my work and make any potential debugging a bit easier.

Line 126 begins Set-DJComputersInSQL. This function accepts, from the pipeline, the kind of object produced by Get-DJOSInfo. It then takes that data and copies it into the database, updating the inventory information. I've used the same basic parameter layout. Here, because I *am* expecting pipeline input, I've used a PROCESS block. I do not expect *this* function to ever be run on its own, and I always want its input coming from the pipeline, so I haven't put the ForEach loop in place – the PROCESS block will be sufficient. I'm again creating Verbose output, and I've piped the output of Invoke-DatabaseQuery to Out-Null. That's because the ExecuteNonQuery() method inside Invoke-DatabaseQuery will normally produce numerical output that indicates success or failure; I don't want to see that output, so Out-Null suppresses it.

Now, close PowerShell, open a new console and give it a whirl.

Testing the New MyTools Module

```
01 PS C:\> import-module mytools
02 PS C:\> Get-DJComputersFromSQL -SQLServer 'localhost\SQLEXPRESS' -
   Database Inventory -Table Computers -Column Computer -verbose | Get-
   DJOSInfo -verbose | Set-DJComputersInSQL -verbose -SQLServer
   'localhost\SQLExpress' -database Inventory -table computers
```

Next, open SQL Server Management Studio. Open a new query window, and see what's in the database.

Examining the Results

```
01 Use [Inventory]
02 Go
03 SELECT * FROM Computers
```

As you did before, click "! Execute" to run this, and you should see a populated data set. Of course, some rows will have missing data because those computers weren't online (or didn't exist) when we ran our test.

Closing Thoughts
This chapter reflects my general thoughts about PowerShell design.

I started with generic, re-usable database functions and made them into a Database module. Those might be used in a huge variety of situations, so saving them into their own module makes them easier to re-use elsewhere.

I then constructed specific functions – Get-DJComputersFromSQL and Set-DJComputersInSQL – to work within the needs of the MyTools module. I made Database a nested module for MyTools, so Database loads transparently and invisibly when MyTools is loaded. Every function is focused on a single, discrete task, and they all work together.

A Final Lesson: Script Design

It's time to start taking some of what you've learned in this book and think about how you'll apply it to the real world. One of the saddest things I see are gigantic, 400-line (or more) PowerShell scripts that implement some complex business process with absolutely no modularization whatsoever. It's wasteful, hard to debug and hard to maintain. Let's take a very real-world task as an example: a new user provisioning script.

A script like this obviously has to perform several tasks, which will differ depending on your environment. Some of those tasks might include:

- Creating the new user account in Active Directory

- Creating a home folder on a file server

- Creating an account on a database server

- Assigning the user to various domain user groups

- Creating an Exchange mailbox

- Assigning the user to various distribution lists

As input, the script might take a bunch of data with new user information: User name, first name, department, last name and so on. But there's no reason such a script has to be one giant entity.

Consider some of the tasks that you're accomplishing. It's foolish to think that those tasks will never, ever, ever be performed outside this provisioning process. Therefore, each task should be modularized. For example, the broad task of "creating a new user account in Active Directory" might actually consist of several sub-tasks:

- Coming up with a random temporary password

- Creating the user account and populating attributes such as department, city, and so forth

- Disabling the user account

- Emailing the temporary password to a special mailbox that your help desk can use to look it up, or perhaps writing it to an Excel spreadsheet.

You could easily make a function to handle these sub-tasks, perhaps naming it something like "New-CoADUser". That "Co" stands for "Company". You'd change that "Co" prefix to something more specific to your company. You could then create functions like that for each of the major tasks that are involved in your provisioning process: "New-CoHomeFolder", "New-CoDBUser", "Set-CoUserGroups" and so forth. Creating a separate function for each of those major tasks has several advantages:

- Each major task could be written by someone else, helping to spread the workload and leverage people's specializations.

- Each major task could be tested and debugged independently, which would make debugging a lot easier.

- Each major task could be used on its own, if needed, or as part of other processes.

Writing each of these tasks as an advanced function would help better document each task's requirements: You simply define well-documented parameters for each piece of information needed to accomplish each task.

All of those task-specific functions would then be saved into a module. Perhaps you'll have a "CompanyTools" module that contained dozens of these functions. Then, your main "new user provisioning script" would simply import that module, load the starting data and call the various task-specific functions – passing along the appropriate starting data to each function's parameters.

There's another advantage to this approach: When you test the task-specific functions on their own, you can manually pass in data to their parameters for testing. *Document* the data you used to test them. That way, if your functions ever fail in the real-world, you can probably assume that the problem relates to the real-world data being passed to the function. You can then examine that data, compare it to your test data, and see what's wrong. Either fix the data, or adjust your function to deal with the data. Be sure to add that "problem data" to your test documentation, so that you test it against any future variations of the function.

This is the *right way* to use PowerShell for complex tasks. It does require a little more design effort up front: You have to *think* about *what you're doing*, break everything down into small pieces and decide what functions to write. You have to think about what data each function will need. That time thinking about the process up front will be well-spent, because it will help you write better, less-buggy functions right from the start.

You can help yourself, and your colleagues, by establishing some organizational standards that everyone uses when writing scripts. For example:

- We will always use Write-Debug to output the contents of variables whenever that content changes, and to output the contents of properties that are being used to make decisions or loops.

- We will always use Write-Verbose before entering a major functional section of a script, inside logical decisions, and inside loops.

- Parameter names will mimic standard names used by PowerShell whenever such prior examples exist.

Establishing standards up front will help everyone on your team produce more consistent code.

Don Jones

Appendix: Best Practices

In the years since Windows PowerShell was introduced, the PowerShell community identified general practices to make scripts easier to write, debug and maintain. It's a good idea to adopt these practices in your own scripting and toolmaking work.

- Avoid Write-Host. As you've learned in this book, there are better alternatives for writing output, verbose information, debug output and so on.

- Avoid setting $ErrorActionPreference. Instead, use the –ErrorAction (or –EA) parameter of a specific command. $ErrorActionPreference is suitable to execute an object method and trap any possible exceptions, but set the preference immediately before executing the method, and then reset the preference afterward.

- Indent your code. As mentioned in this book, nicely formatted code is easier to read, understand, follow and debug.

- Spell out cmdlet and parameter names in their entirety. This helps improve readability and clarity.

- Don't use "Hungarian notation" for variable names, such as $strComputerName. It's less important to track the type of object in a variable, and more important to create clarity. This is especially true for parameters, where names should be consistent with those of other commands.

- Rely more on Write-Verbose to provide inline documentation of what your script is doing. Use inline comments only when you need to document something *only* for another scripter, since comments are harder to surface for someone *using* the script.

- Use single quotation marks unless you explicitly need the special features of double quotation marks.

- Use a source control solution to manage versions of your scripts. Some higher-end PowerShell editors, such as PrimalScript Studio and PowerGUI Pro, include integrated source control features.

- Use a code-signing certificate to sign completed scripts.

- Name scripts and functions using cmdlet-style, Verb-Noun naming. Apply a 2- or 3-character prefix to the noun to relate each script or function to your organization.

- Avoid modifying or relying on the global scope, particularly for variables.

- Output objects – never text.

Don Jones

Made in the USA
Lexington, KY
26 April 2012